The Kid-Friendly Dad

Connecting with Your Kids in a Chaotic World

With Ideas for Kid-Friendly Moms

FRANK MARTIN

INTERVARSITY PRESS
DOWNERS GROVE, ILLINOIS 60515

InterVarsity Press® is the book-publishing division of InterVarsity Christian Fellowship®, a student movement active on campus at hundreds of universities, colleges and schools of nursing in the United States of America, and a member movement of the International Fellowship of Evangelical Students. For information about local and regional activities, write Public Relations Dept., InterVarsity Christian Fellowship, 6400 Schroeder Rd., P.O. Box 7895, Madison, WI 53707-7895.

All Scripture quotations, unless otherwise indicated, are taken from the HOLY BIBLE, NEW INTERNATIONAL VERSION®. NIV®. Copyright ©1973, 1978, 1984 by International Bible Society. Used by permission of Zondervan Publishing House. All rights reserved.

Cover photograph: Jim Whitmer

ISBN 0-8308-1632-1

Printed in the United States of America ∞

Library of Congress Cataloging-in-Publication Data

Martin, Frank. 1958-
    The kid-friendly dad: connecting with your kids in a chaotic
    world/Frank Martin.
        p.   cm.
    Includes bibliographical references.
    ISBN 0-8308-1632-1
    1. Fatherhood.   2. Fathers and daughters.   3. Fathers and sons.
    4. Parenting.   I. Title.
HQ756.M348   1993
306.874'2—dc20   93-42737
                                                                                      CIP

15   14   13   12   11   10   9   8   7   6   5   4   3   2   1
05   04   03   02   01   00   99   98   97   96   95   94

To Ruthie,
the world's most
husband-friendly wife

Acknowledgments

One of the best parts of writing a book (besides, of course, seeing your name on the cover!) is getting to meet a lot of new friends along the way. Please applaud along with me as I thank some of the great people who helped this idea come to fruition.

To Cynthia Bunch-Hotaling—the editor so nice they named her twice. I think she worked as hard on this book as I did. Thanks for your skill and insight and encouragement.

To Andy Le Peau and the staff at InterVarsity. Thanks for believing in me and this project. (By the way, I have this idea for another book I'd like to bounce off you . . .)

To Jerry Jenkins, the "Grand Poobah" of publishing. More than anyone, he has gone out of his way to help me in my writing career. Thanks for everything. (And I still owe you dinner.)

To my kid-friendly parents, Walter and Veronika Martin, for showing me how unconditional love can be. Thanks, and I love you.

To Bob and Doris Vance, the best in-laws marriage can buy. Thanks for your kind words and encouragement.

To my wonderful, perfect kids, David and Kandilyn. "You need to write a book about me and Mommy and Kandilyn and how much you love us," David told me. So I did. Thanks for being patient with me during the process.

And, of course, to my wife, Ruthie, the best pre-editor a writer can have. This book would not have happened without her. Your love makes me a better husband, a kinder father and a more committed Christian. Not to mention a happier man! Thanks for being my best friend.

One last note of sincere gratitude: To Mrs. Jackson, my tenth-grade English teacher, for lighting a fire that never went out. God bless you, you molder of dreams.

—1—
The Kid-Friendly Dad

*T*HE KID-FRIENDLY DAD KNOWS HOW TO BE MUCH MORE THAN *a father. He can be a shepherd, consultant, adviser, counselor, teacher, model, anchor, beacon and friend.*

"I just don't know what else to do. It seems the harder I try, the worse things get."

Bill leaned across the table, staring into the bottom of his half-empty cup of coffee. His eyes looked weary, his face somber. His voice sounded beaten and defeated.

"If I only knew what I was doing wrong, I could fix it. But I don't. I'm doing everything I know how to do, and it never seems to be enough."

He leaned back in his chair and sighed deeply. "Sometimes I wonder if it's all worth it. I know this sounds terrible, but maybe I should have never had kids. Maybe I just wasn't cut out to be a father."

Bill and I had met for lunch before, and we had often talked of the problems he was having with his sons, but today was different. Today he seemed more distant, more confused, more broken and fatigued. Like a man with the life drained out of him.

"Things just aren't like they used to be. If I had talked to my father the way Timmy talks to me, I'd have never lived to see twenty. I wouldn't have dared even to think about it." He lifted his head, aiming his gaze in my direction. "So what have I done to let Timmy think he can talk to me that way? I'm not doing anything different than my father used to do. Is it me, or have kids changed that much over the last thirty years?"

He glanced down at his cup for a second, then again gazed upward. "I'm at the end of my rope. I really can't take it anymore. I'm ready to just throw up my hands and give in."

I wanted to have an answer for Bill. I wanted to lean forward with a smile, take a pen and a napkin and outline a ten-step program of parenting guaranteed to put his family problems behind him. I wanted to take his dilemma and wrap it up neatly inside a few words of wisdom, pat him on the back and send him home with renewed confidence. "You just follow this plan and everything will work out fine," I wanted to tell him. "Let me know if I can be of any more help to you."

But I didn't say anything. I couldn't. I just sat and listened, trying desperately to think of some words of encouragement.

We finished our coffee, Bill thanked me for listening, and I drove home wishing I could have been more help. What Bill needed I wasn't able to give to him. He needed a concrete answer to his problems, not a pat on the back and a kind word. He needed rules to parent by, not clichés to get him through the day. He needed wisdom—clear-cut guidance and direction. He needed what we all need.

What's a Father to Do?

Parenting is an inexact science, to say the least. There is no job on earth more demanding and confusing than taking tiny, helpless souls at birth and seeing them through to adulthood. Molding their little minds and shaping their hearts. Tending daily to their physical and spiritual needs. Trying to balance a healthy amount of discipline with a generous amount of freedom and independence. Teaching them to have strong self-esteem but also humility.

Bill isn't alone in his struggles. More and more fathers today are feeling those same feelings of inadequacy, and the answers seem as elusive as ever.

What about you? What would you have said to Bill over cold coffee that afternoon in the diner? Maybe you could have offered a few insights that neither of us could find. Perhaps you could have sent him home with a renewed determination and a concrete plan of action.

Or perhaps not. Maybe instead you would have joined him in his anguish. Maybe you, too, have been stumped by the task of keeping your children in line. You, too, have questions about what your kids need in a dad.

Maybe you, too, have stood shaken and distraught at the anger aimed in your direction by your child. You've been on the business end of a sharp and unbridled tongue once too often, and now you are finding yourself lying awake at night, wondering what you've done wrong.

Or maybe you're a new father. You thought you could handle anything parenting could throw at you, but now you find yourself completely baffled by your inability to relate to your three-year-old daughter.

You understand much better than you wished what Bill was going through. And you're looking daily for the same answers.

I share Bill's story to let you know that you're not alone. Your feelings of uncertainty mirror those of millions of fathers across the country. We've all wondered at times if we were really cut out to be parents.

Finding a Plan of Action

I often wonder how things have turned out for Bill. I wish I could sit across the table from him one more time, staring into those lost and empty eyes. Not because I now have all the answers to the questions parents ask, but because I have some new ideas I'd like to share with him. I have some thoughts about what kids need most from their dads that I'd like him to hear. And I have a list of fatherly attributes—a concrete plan of action for dads—that I'd like to scribble on a napkin for him. They wouldn't be meant to solve all his problems, but they would give him some direction and guidance. They would give him something to strive for. I know he'd be interested in listening.

Since you've chosen to lay down your hard-earned money for this book, you, too, must be interested in listening. You, too, must have your questions about what it takes to be a good father. If I'm right, then read on and let's explore it together. But first, let me give you a preview of our trip—a road map, so to speak.

I'll start by telling you what this book is about. It's about learning to be the kind of father that God expects of a man. It's about becoming the kind of dad that your kids will look up to and emulate—not because they are told to, but because they really *want* to. It's about learning to fit into the many hats a father must wear in today's high-tech, low-morals society. And it's about learning to listen to your kids—letting them tell you what they need from you. Listening not just with your ears, but with your senses and your heart—through feelings, eye contact, intuition and prayer.

I should also tell you what this book is *not* about. It's not about what our kids should do to grow up spiritually healthy. It's about learning to become a father. It's about *our* lives, not our kids'. It's about *our* spiritual health, not our children's. It's about overcoming *our* inadequacies as parents and leaders, not their inabilities to follow.

There's one other thing this book is not. It's not a concrete set of rules to parent by, guaranteed to keep your kids healthy, wealthy, spiritual and wise. I don't believe such a list exists, though many have formulated what they believe to be the absolute, be-all and end-all formula for parenting.

I like to remind myself of the proverbial story of the author-turned-father-turned-parenting expert. When his son was two months old, he wrote his first child-rearing book entitled *Rules for Raising Spiritual Kids*. When his son turned two, he updated the volume and changed the title to *Guidelines for Parents of Young Children*. Some years later he rewrote the book entirely and called it *Helpful Suggestions for Struggling Parents*. It's true: the longer we are parents, the less likely we are to follow formulas.

Before I was married, I remember giving my older brother advice on dealing with his son. He turned to me and said, "The only people I know who are experts on raising kids are those who don't have any." Boy, was he right!

This book does not presume to be a one-size-fits-all book of parenting. In fact, were the title not already in place, I could easily retitle it as *Helpful Suggestions for Struggling Fathers*. Perhaps a footnote below the title would read, *And Soon-to-Be-Struggling Fathers,* as well.

As Christian fathers, we're all in this together. We all make mistakes. We all have our good points. And most important, we all want our kids to grow up spiritually strong. The trouble is, we sometimes forget the impact our example and lifestyle have on them and their future. We often assume that if we are there to answer their questions and give them good counsel and advice, they will not stray. We assume that they will make it through the tough and doubting times the same way we did as young adults.

We assume too much.

A Father for the Nineties

Times have changed, but too often, fathers haven't. Too often we try to relate to our kids the same way our parents related to us. It usually doesn't work.

Our children are not growing up in the same world we grew up in. The forces that pull at them daily are more powerful and anti-Christian than many of us ever had to face. They themselves know it. Their peers know it. Their teachers know it. Their youth ministers know it. But often, their parents don't.

Being a father in the nineties means having to face and deal with problems that most of our fathers could have never imagined having to deal with. How many of our fathers ever had to warn us of the dangers of Satanism? How many of us ever had to make a decision about drugs before high school—much less in the third, fourth or fifth grade? When I was in ninth grade, I could count on one hand the girls and boys in my class who were "sexually active"—or who even knew much about it.

And those are just the problems we all see on the surface. Many of their struggles are more subtle and confusing—the mixed messages they get from sex and violence on television; the humanistic approach to education that counters everything they've been taught at home; the lack of moral guidance in the community, school and government; the eggshells they walk on daily due to the "politically correct" environment they are forced to live in; the pressure girls face from the backlash of the "women's movement"; the influx of cultic ideals and theories brought on by the New Age movement; and on and on. Just trying to keep up with the changes in society is enough to make you weary. Try putting yourself in the shoes of your impressionable children, as they work through the confusion of their most formative years deep in the midst of it all. It's enough to send any good ostrich running for the sandbox.

Those are just a few of the struggles they face as children. And as their fathers, we need to face their struggles with them. To grow as their world changes. To adapt our style of leadership to meet the needs of the time. To try as much as possible, to be all of the things they need—to become all things to our children—in order to help them navigate the stormy seas of modern-day childhood and adolescence.

That's what a kid-friendly dad is. A man who knows how to be much more than a father. He is one who can be a shepherd, consultant, adviser, counselor, teacher, model, anchor, beacon and friend.

It's a tough calling, but one that even you and I can achieve. If, of course, we are willing to try.

—2—
Father-in-Residence

*U*NLESS WE ARE WILLING TO GIVE OF OUR TIME AND EN-
*ergy—to become a father-in-residence instead of a dad-
from-a-distance—we will never be the kind of father our
kids need and deserve.*

Colorado is a beautiful place to live any time of the year, but in the
winter it is nothing short of breathtaking. This morning, like many
other mornings, we woke up to a ten-inch blanket of snow covering
the earth. From tree branches to fences to rooftops, as far as we could
see the world was fresh and white.

Our breakfast window frames the Rocky Mountains, with Pike's
Peak towering above them all in the distance. Today they are covered
with white caps of snow. It is a truly majestic view to behold. This, I
thought to myself, is why we moved to Colorado.

But that was breakfast.

Now it is nearly noon, and I've just come in from spending a good part of the morning shoveling snow off of everything from the front porch to the driveway to the sidewalk, and once again I'm wondering if it was worth the trouble.

For the fourth time in less than a week, I was forced to don my gloves, coat and snow boots and brave the damp cold to clear the walkways. To many, this is not that large of a task. But we live on a corner lot—the largest one on the block. Our sidewalk starts on one end of the house, runs the length of the curb to the corner, turns and stretches halfway down the next street. A great deal of sidewalk area, mind you. It's a good selling point, but on days like today I'm tempted to relinquish those bragging rights to the first bidder.

We're also stuck in the house for the most part. This kind of weather turns driving into a contact sport, so I had to put off several errands until later in the afternoon.

As beautiful as the snow is, the drawbacks are very definite. But it's a tradeoff we have to live with. That is, if we want to live in Colorado.

Life is filled with tradeoffs. My wife enjoys fresh vegetables in the summer. She doesn't particularly enjoy gardening, but she knows that if she wants freshly grown vegetables, it's something she must do. So every spring, she plants her garden—knowing full well the work that it will entail over the next few months. It's a tradeoff she's willing to make.

In business, there are also tradeoffs. The business I run is very time-demanding. I could work twenty-four hours a day and never do everything I'd like to make it grow and flourish. I could cut back on staff, take on added responsibilities myself, and perhaps bring home a larger share of the profits. But I don't. I delegate. I set my hours the way I want them to be set. I hire out work, even though I could do it myself, and I go home instead. My most important work, I've decided, is right here—spending time with my wife and kids.

Am I ambitious? Absolutely. Overambitious, if anything. But I've made a decision. It's a tradeoff. I'd rather spend time at home, being a father and a husband, than live in a bigger house, drive a nicer car, and entertain more important clients. The sacrifice (if you consider it that) is one I am willing to make.

Making Choices

Look at your own life for a minute. Think of the tradeoffs that you make on a daily basis. When buying a car, you have to decide what part of your time and income you are willing to put into a car. If you spend a lot on it, some other purchase might have to wait. If you spend less on it, you might not get the car you want. If you live in a snowy state like we do, you will have to decide between the luxury of a nice family car, or the practicality of a rugged-riding four-wheel-drive for the winter months.

Tradeoffs are everywhere, in every avenue and corner of our lives. And we all must live with them.

The most interesting thing about tradeoffs, however, is how they reveal where our affections lie. They tend to say volumes about what is and isn't important to us. They give one of the clearest pictures on earth of what treasures are truly at the root of a man's heart. There is no more telling measure of a man's true priorities than what he chooses to spend his money and time on.

Show me a man with a garage full of new tools, old auto parts and up-to-date owner's manuals, and I'll show you a man who's in love with his car.

Give me a man with a high-profile job, a five-digit mortgage payment and a briefcase full of frequent-flier cards, and I'll show you a family that's feeling more than a little neglected.

A simple stroll through any man's list of assets will tell you more about him than he probably wants you to know.

Children, too, have an innate ability to sense what is important to their parents. They see the choices we make on a daily basis, and every decision is registered and filed away in their minds. It doesn't take them long to get a clear picture of our priority list.

More important, they see clearly where they fall on that list. And in today's fast-paced, success-oriented society, they often fall much further down the list than they should.

A Matter of Priority

My father retired from the military when I was ten. His pension was small and the cost of living was rising quickly, but because of a disability he could not take on an additional job. So he retired. And we learned to budget well.

As a result, I can remember having my father around the house more than most of my friends. He was always there for us when we needed him.

I used to wonder why he didn't start developing a long list of hobbies or join some retirement clubs to give himself something to do and somewhere to go for relaxation. Most fathers do when they retire. But mine didn't. Instead he threw himself into our lives. He took on extra chores around the house, remodeled the bedroom closets and looked for ways to spend more time with us.

It never seemed to bother him that while most men his age were developing "power friendships" and working toward bigger paychecks, he was spending his days at home helping to raise his kids. The task came naturally to him, and he thrived on it. Our worries became his worries, our triumphs his triumphs, our world his world.

Today when I reflect on my youth, the things I remember are near and dear to me. I remember fishing trips where Dad spent the entire day untangling lines, baiting hooks and wading knee-deep in water to retrieve snagged lures. We never caught many fish, but we always went back.

I remember strapping on a carpenter's belt and following Dad into the back yard to work on a table or cabinet he was building. Often, I would cut a board too short or hammer a nail where it didn't belong, and he would have to go out of his way to fix my mistakes. Sometimes that meant scratching the project altogether and starting over. But he took it in stride. My learning how to build always seemed more important to him than the lost time and wasted wood.

During those years, my father was sending a clear message to our family about what was important to him. We never once wondered about where we fell on his priority list. We knew instinctively that we—and Mom—were at the very top.

Though we never thought about it, Dad was making a tradeoff. There were many things, I'm sure, he would have liked to accomplish during his retirement years. But he put his dreams and ambitions on hold and instead spent his time with us. It was a tradeoff he was willing to make.

When Priorities Are in the Wrong Order

In contrast to my father, I know a man who, when faced with a similar decision, decided that his work should come first. It was important to him that his kids grow up with the things he never had a child. He truly loved his children and wanted them to have the best of everything. And they did. They went to the finest schools, wore the latest fashions and drove the nicest cars around. But the tradeoff was obvious. They grew up with their father at arm's length. They could usually reach him by phone if they wanted to talk with him about their day. And he always took their calls—unless, of course, he was in a meeting or on the phone with a client.

It bothered him that he wasn't spending more time with his family, but he knew that it had to be done if they were to maintain their standard of living. His kids knew he loved them, and that, he thought, was the important thing.

Today his family life is in a shambles. His marriage is over and his kids are distant. But his business is still doing well.

He recently confided that if he had the decision to make all over again, he would make a different choice. He could easily live without the money, he says, if only things could be different with his family.

What he knows now that he didn't know then is that his children

had a different view of his business involvement. While he
thought he was showing his love
through the things he provided,
they had concluded that he didn't
want to spend time with them.
They saw themselves being
placed far down the page on his
list of priorities. So they went on
with their lives without him, wondering what they had done to
alienate their father.

It's a sad story, but an all-too-

> *"A* Newsweek *article reported that
> middle-class American fathers
> spend an average of fifteen to
> twenty minutes per day with their
> children. In many cases, even if the
> fathers are present physically, they
> are absent relationally. We need
> men who will place their families
> as the number one priority in their
> lives. Men who will give as much
> of themselves to their children as
> they do to their work."*
>
> —*James A. Harnish, reprinted from* Chris-
> tian Home, *June 1977, p. 23.*

common one. Fathers of the twentieth century are forced to decide
how much of their time will be dedicated to the office and how much
will be spent at home. We are caught between society's view of
success and our children's need for a hands-on dad. Too often we make
the wrong choices.

I have many fond memories of childhood and time spent with my
father. They've given me a direction and security in life that I could
have never had without his involvement. And I credit those experiences as the basis for my own decision to spend time with my family
rather than working toward building a larger business.

What Kids Need Most

Parenting takes time. It takes commitment and sacrifice—even more
today than in days gone by. Josh McDowell likes to say that children
spell *love* differently from their parents. They spell it T-I-M-E. He's
right.

But they're not thinking about what we've come to call "quality
time." They're thinking of quantity.

Tim Hansel wrote about "quality time" in *What Kids Need Most in
a Dad:*

When we start using terms and images such as "quality time" we begin to devalue the intrinsic wonder of life itself.

Life is time-consuming. Time is the very crucible of fathering. The most profound way I let my family know I love them is by giving them time. Of course I want that time to have elements of quality in it . . . but at the bottom line there is no substitute for the wonder of time itself.[1]

Pollster Louis Harris has said, "Time may have become the most precious commodity in the land." It is one thing there never seems to be enough of.

In 1965, testimony before a Senate subcommittee claimed that by 1985, Americans would be working twenty-two hours a week and would be able to retire at age thirty-eight. Why such optimism? Computers. The computer age, they predicted, would create such advances in technology that people could do ten times the work in half the time. Standards of living would easily be met on a part-time work schedule.

> **Five Major Time Wasters in the Home**
>
> *1. Television. Nothing has gobbled up more time than the one-eyed monster that resides in most living rooms around the country.*
>
> *2. Newspapers and magazines. I enjoy my afternoon reading as much as the next person. But if my children feel left out, my reading time must go.*
>
> *3. Unnecessary housework. An old professor used to refute the saying "If it's worth doing, it's worth doing right." He would reply, "I can think of a lot of things worth doing that are not worth doing right—like ironing and folding bedsheets." We all want to keep a clean house, but we don't need to let it become an obsession. Time with our children is more important.*
>
> *4. Personal hobbies. An enjoyable hobby can be good for us, but not if we're constantly using it to get away from the wife and kids. Let's use hobbies to get our kids involved with the family, not to escape.*
>
> *5. Catching up on office work. "Wait a minute—that's not a waste of time!" you might say. But it certainly does take time that could be spent with your kids. We all have to use our own time to catch up on occasion, but we should see that it remains the exception rather than the rule.*

As we know, it didn't work out that way. In fact, the opposite has happened. What used to be a standard forty-hour work week has now become for many a forty-eight-hour week. We're working more, not less. In theory, new technology should have produced the end result many predicted, but they forgot to figure in one important part of the formula: man's ambition and insatiable desire for more. In spite of the computer age, the average amount of leisure time has shrunk thirty-seven percent since 1973.[2]

"I've got so many irons in the fire, I can't keep any of them hot," complained one young father.

Can't we all relate?

Breaking from the Circle

Something has got to give. Somewhere in the midst of all the hustle and bustle of life and work and worry, our children need our attention more than ever. Their worlds, too, are being kicked into fast-forward by the business of the twentieth century, and they often have a harder time adapting than we think.

I like to use the illustration of an experiment conducted by Jean Henri Fabre, the great French entomologist. He took a number of processionary caterpillars—so named because they always marched in militarylike formation—and lined them around the inner edge of a flowerpot until they formed a complete, unending circle. For three days he monitored them as they marched around and around the edge of the flowerpot, never once breaking the circle. At the end of the third day, he placed several pine needles—the food of processionary caterpillars—in the center of the pot. For four more days and nights, the caterpillars marched in a circle. Eventually they dropped dead from starvation and exhaustion.

They had been walking less than six inches from food, and yet one by one, they starved to death. For seven days and nights they marched, and never once did any of them leave the circle to eat.

We men can be a lot like that, can't we? We get busy doing the things we do, marching behind all of the other success-oriented caterpillars, never knowing that all the while the one thing in our lives that we need so badly—our family—sits unnoticed just inches away.

That's a lesson I need to remember. I've spent too many long evenings working in my office trying to meet a deadline while my wife and kids play on the floor of the family den. Working out of the home has its advantages, but it also brings with it the temptation to work through the evening instead of dealing with the deadlines later. It's easy to get caught up in the march toward success, forgetting the ones who need me most.

Becoming a Father-in-Residence

If you spend your life marching around the edges of your flower-potted world, but really going nowhere, I encourage you to break free from the circle. Take off your blinders and see the world around you.

A kid-friendly dad, above all else, knows what should and shouldn't be important in his life. He knows how to keep his priorities in proper order. He knows the tradeoffs that must be made in order to be the kind of father that his kids need, and is more than willing to make the sacrifices.

A kid-friendly dad is willing to be a father-in-residence. He knows that his kids need a father who is there for them when they need him—physically as well as emotionally.

Your kids need a father who will take them on his lap and hold them against his chest as they talk about the day's events before bedtime—not one who says goodnight over the phone

> **Out of the Mouths of Babes!**
> *A young mother was explaining to her inquisitive first-grader why Daddy had to work so hard. The child had been noticing her father coming home late in the evenings with a briefcase full of paperwork, and then retiring to his study where he continued working long after bedtime.*
>
> *"Daddy is just a very busy man," Mom explained. "And he has more work to do than he can get done at the office."*
>
> *The daughter cocked her head, raised an eyebrow and said, "Then why don't they put him in a slower group?"*
>
> *(I wonder how many of us belong in a "slower group"!)*

while he "ties up some loose ends" at work.

Your kids need a father who will decorate the house and blow up balloons for their upcoming birthday party—not one who sends a ten-dollar bill and a card from another business trip he "really wished he could have gotten out of this time."

Your kids need to know that they hold the top spot on your list of priorities. And that nothing else even comes close.

Time is a precious commodity—both to you and to your kids. And it is slipping away daily. Don't wait until it's too late. Spend some time with your children. Spend some time with your wife. Spend some time with God. Take a good hard look at your list of priorities, and rearrange it accordingly.

Not all of us can spend the kind of time with our kids that my father was able to spend with us, but we can at least let them know where they stand among our list of treasures. I'm willing to bet that there's not a father among us who couldn't find more time to spend with his kids if he really tried. I know I could. And if you're honest with yourself, you probably could too.

Without any doubt, this has to be the first and most important step in becoming a kid-friendly dad. Unless we are willing to give of our time and energy—to become a father-in-residence instead of a dad-from-a-distance—we will never be the kind of father our kids need and deserve. It's the one ingredient in the formula you can't leave out.

A MESSAGE FOR KID-FRIENDLY MOMS

Nothing makes me want to put more time and energy into my home life than seeing my wife make that same effort. It's inspiring to watch her take time out of her busy schedule to take the kids to the park or sit down with them on the floor of their rooms to play for an hour. She also makes time to sit out on the deck with me after a busy afternoon and talk about the day's events.

When it's apparent that the kids and I top her list of priorities, it reminds me daily to keep my priorities in order as well.

As a wife, you will be doing your husband and kids an invaluable service by looking for ways to show them how important they are to you.

No task on earth should come before your husband and children—whether it's running a business, working on the school board, heading up a church ministry or participating in a social club. Your children need your time and attention as much as they need their father's—sometimes more.

You'll be surprised what an inspiration it is to your husband when he sees you putting all the energy you've got into making your house a home!

—3—
Spiritual
Shepherd

*W*HEN ALL IS SAID AND DONE, THERE IS NO MORE IMPORTANT *task on earth than seeing that your children fall in love with the Lord. This is the ultimate goal of every Christian parent—to get to heaven, and to see that your family gets there with you.*

I had just settled into my office chair at five this evening to catch up on some work when my wife, Ruthie, called to me from the kitchen. She needed me to watch the kids while she took dinner to a sick friend. I halfheartedly gathered them together in the den, where they played on the floor as I tried to catch some of the evening news. No sooner had I sat down than the phone rang. It was one of my clients—an important one.

Just then four-year-old David jumped up from the floor and stepped on the toes of Kandilyn, our one-year-old.

"Waaaaaaaah!"

I held the phone with one hand, tried to comfort her with the other and hoped that my client wasn't hearing the full extent of the chaos. I put him on hold, set Kandilyn on the couch and ran to my office to finish the call. Through the entire conversation I could hear David running and shouting through the house, his voice fading then growing as he tore through the halls. All the while, Kandilyn shrieked louder and higher by the minute.

When Ruthie came home a half hour later, we gathered around the table for supper. David led the prayer, thanking God for Mommy and Daddy and Kandilyn and Jesus and everybody. I realized that he had forgotten to thank God for the food, but I was too stressed and hungry to remind him. We then proceeded with our daily ritual of threatening, begging and bribing the kids to eat and sit still at the same time (an art that seems to be beyond the realm of possibility for children).

After dinner, we settled back into the den, where Ruthie and I tried unsuccessfully to have a much-needed conversation amidst the noise and confusion. We were tired. The kids were loud. The phone kept ringing. The kids got louder. The toy box was empty and the den was a wreck. And soon, everyone was tense and on edge.

At eight sharp, we started getting the kids ready for bed. Ruthie tucked Kandilyn into her crib while I prayed with David. We normally sing a few songs, recite some verses from memory and share a Bible story, but tonight we didn't. I was tired and David didn't mention it, so I hugged him and turned off the lights.

It is now nine, and I'm once again settling into my office chair—this time to tackle the task of writing about the need for fathers to shepherd their children spiritually. After tonight, I'm wondering seriously how much business I have writing on the subject in the first place. Nights like this do not occur every day, but they do happen. And I always feel bad afterward.

Getting to the Bottom Line

What does it mean to be a "spiritual shepherd" in your home? How does a father tend to the spiritual needs of his kids amidst work and worry and chaos? Where does a man find the time and energy to make a difference in his children's spiritual development when he can barely maintain his own relationship with God?

If you're a Christian and a father, you've no doubt asked those kinds of questions. If you worry about your kids as much as I do, you've probably asked them often.

For me, being a spiritual shepherd is the bottom line. It's where the rubber meets the road. When all is said and done, there is no more important task on earth than seeing that your children fall in love with the Lord. This is the ultimate goal of every Christian parent—to get to heaven, and to see that your family gets there with you. What task could possibly pull more weight than this one?

The real question is, how do we do that? How do we help our kids develop a relationship with God? And how do we help them maintain that relationship when they do find it?

The Power of Modeling

Jorie Kincaid has summed up in one word what she believes to be the single most important factor in the spiritual development of children: modeling.

In her book *The Power of Modeling* she writes:

Modeling shifts my primary focus as a parent from doing to being. If my children watch me, they will probably become very much like me. This means that my identity is very important. . . . Our success or failure in modeling is not dependent on our perfect behavior. Rather, the success of modeling is dependent on being a parent who desires to be like Christ through the ups and downs of life. Modeling works when we are willing to allow God to take over where we are weak and inadequate.[1]

I couldn't agree more. I've seen the principle at work again and again in my own family. It often scares me to see how closely my kids emulate me—in every area of life.

I'm not particularly fond of vegetables. In fact, I'd just as soon fill my plate with a good serving of meat and leave the greens for everyone else. But I've had to learn (at the prodding of my wife) that what I'm doing is setting a bad example for the kids. We now have to bribe David to get him to eat his vegetables, even though we know he likes them. He has liked them since he was a baby. But he has seen me shun them in the past, and has picked up on it.

It's sobering to think of the great influence our habits and actions—both good and bad—will have on the lives of our children. And nowhere is this more important than in the area of spirituality.

If I am ever to expect my children to grow in love for the Lord, I must first see that my life exudes that quality. If I want my children to learn the joy of Christian living, I must first learn to be a joyful Christian. If I want my children to look to God for guidance in their lives, I must let them see me on my knees daily asking God for guidance in mine.

The spiritual development of my children's lives begins and ends with the depth of my own relationship with God. There is no greater lesson a father could learn.

> When it comes to spiritually equipping our children, there is no better formula than the one outlined in Deuteronomy 6:4-9:
>
> *Hear, O Israel: The LORD our God, the LORD is one. Love the LORD your God with all your heart and with all your soul and with all your strength. These commandments that I give you today are to be upon your hearts. Impress them on your children. Talk about them when you sit at home and when you walk along the road, when you lie down and when you get up. Tie them as symbols on your hands and bind them on your foreheads. Write them on the doorframes of your houses and on your gates.*

Proactive Shepherding

Even so, there is more to modeling spirituality than just being spiritual. It's not enough to feel comfortable with our own relationship with God; we must also see that our kids understand and witness the depth of that relationship. And in order for that to happen, we must look for ways to demonstrate our faith to them. Being a spiritual shepherd means learning to be proactive, not just reactive. It means looking for ways to model your values and beliefs for your children.

There are many ways to demonstrate your love for Christ to your family. You've probably developed a few of your own. But I'd like to share with you some of the ways I feel strongly about—concrete things we can do to show clearly the important role Christ plays in our lives.

1. *Set aside a time for your own private daily devotions.* For years preachers have been telling Christians to set aside an hour a day for private devotions. It's more than a good idea—it's a biblical principle. But to many, it seems so unrealistic. Who has an extra hour to burn? We already need another six hours each day just to finish our to-do list.

Even so, the idea must not be so easily dismissed. If we don't have an hour a day to give to God, how serious can we be when we say we've committed our lives to his cause? If we've truly surrendered "all to Jesus," is it asking too much to reflect on his will for an hour? The truth is, an hour is inadequate at best.

But just as important as the impact daily devotions has on our lives is the impact it will have on our children. They need to see clearly our willingness to spend time to reflect on God.

Some years back, when David was two, Ruthie started having a one-hour daily devotional. She called it her "quiet time." During that hour David was to stay clear of our bedroom. A few weeks later I walked into David's room one afternoon to find him sitting on his bed with a small Bible open in his hands.

"Don't come in, Daddy," he told me.

"Why can't I come in?" I asked.

"Because I'm having my quiet time."

If you think kids don't pick up quickly on their parents' habits, then you probably don't have kids.

2. *Set aside a time for family devotions.* I'm surprised and saddened at the growing trend away from regular family devotions. Several recent books on parenting have called the idea "forced" and "boring" and "ineffective." These authors believe that children are turned off

rather than uplifted by family devotions.

I don't agree. At young ages, children love to sing and pray and hear Bible stories. Though I realize that at certain ages boredom will set in, boredom is no reason to stop meeting. At these critical ages kids need spiritual influences the most. And they most need to see the depth of their parents' commitment.

If you want to start traditions in your family that will make a lasting impact on your children's future, start a time of daily, family devotions while they're young.

3. *Use mealtimes to your advantage.* Think for a moment about the dynamics of family mealtimes. The entire family is seated together in a tight circle, each facing inward. It's like a mini-board-meeting twice a day. How sad that so many of these times are wasted arguing, watching TV on the side or chewing in silence. I can't imagine a better time and place for parents to implement good spiritual ideas and discussions.

I came from a big family, and I remember mealtime as the best hour of every day. It was a time of bonding, praying together and sharing our thoughts.

Sitting around our large dining-room table, we learned things about our parents that would have been lost otherwise. Many of our meals ended hours after the food

Ideas for Creating a Meaningful Family Devotional Time

■ *Make a list of praise songs that your children enjoy singing. Then have family members take turns telling what good thing God has done for them that day. After telling their praise story, they get to pick a song from the list and lead the group in singing it.*

■ *Have one child sit in the middle of the room while everyone takes turn saying what they appreciate most about him or her.*

■ *Have the children read their favorite Bible verse and explain why it means so much to them.*

■ *Instead of preparing a lesson each day, use the time to read through books of the Bible, a few verses at a time. You'll be surprised at how much your children get out of it.*

■ *Keep a running prayer list that you bring out at each devotion time. Add new prayer needs to the list, and remember to thank God for prayers he has answered.*

was cold as we listened intently to stories about my mother's child-hood in war-torn Germany and my father's boyhood days in the backwoods of Louisiana. We never tired of hearing how these two souls who grew up worlds apart came to meet and marry.

Some say that family mealtimes are a thing of the past—part of an era that once was but can be no more. True, the fast-paced, take-out mentality of the twentieth century has made long family mealtimes a rarity. But we don't have to let these wonderful times of bonding be lost. Buy a big table and surround it with comfortable chairs. And use mealtimes to your advantage.

4. *When you pray with your children, pray honestly and sincerely.* Some time ago while teaching a Sunday-school class of two-year-olds, I was struck by the different reactions the children had to prayer. When it came time to pray, each took on a different stance or position. Little Joel Brown, the son of our youth minister, would immediately lean forward on the edge of his chair, close his eyes into a tight squint and fold his hands together in front of his forehead. He appeared to be as deep into thought and meditation as any adult I've seen. It wasn't hard to see what bedtime prayers were like at his house.

Other kids would simply fold their hands in their laps and become very still and quiet. Still others would become active and disinterested the minute the prayer began. I knew that with very few exceptions, prayer was a regular practice in these kids' homes. And yet, each had his or her own idea about what prayer was.

How we pray at home says volumes to our kids about our relation-ship with God. Though I'm not advocating formal, stoic prayers sprinkled with "thee's" and "thou's," I do think we need to impress on our kids the importance of what we're doing. If they don't sense that prayer time is special to us, it won't be special to them.

I recently found myself wondering about the message my kids were getting about our nightly prayer time together. I sensed that our prayers were becoming repetitious and ritualistic. So one night I suggested that we kneel on the edge of the bed and fold our hands—something people don't seem to do much anymore. Though Kandilyn was too young to understand what was going on, David loved it. Now he wants to kneel every night. It's a simple, arguably unimportant thing, but it makes the time more meaningful. And it makes talking to God seem that much more important.

5. *Look for opportunities to model good values.* As Christians, we've all learned to do our good deeds in secret, to keep our left hand from knowing what our right hand is doing. The principle is biblical. But when it comes to our kids, I think they need to see the sacrifices their parents make. They need to know that their parents are decent, compassionate people.

For the last few months, our family has been taking supper several times a week to a sick friend and his family. We don't do it for glory or praise; we just saw a need and started filling it. Most of our friends will never know anything about it.

Still, we feel that it is good for the kids to see us reaching out to those who are hurting. We make a point of taking the kids with us on occasion. We also include this family in our prayers daily.

We should never underestimate the great impact it makes on kids when they see their parents living a life of consistent, Christian values.

6. *Let them see you take a stand.* When is the last time you had to stand up for what you believe? Have you had to face any Goliaths lately?

On a day-to-day level, Christian adults in America don't often have to take a tough stand on issues. When our values or beliefs are challenged, it is usually more subtle than threatening. And it's easy to simply remain quiet when we sense a confrontation coming on. I often do.

But our kids don't have it so easy. From an early age, children are forced into confrontations. The third-grade bullies challenge them on the playground every time the teachers turn their backs; the sixth-grade "foul-mouths" tease them for being a "momma's boy"; the tenth-grade dealers call them "chicken" if they refuse their wares; the twelfth-grade athletes make fun of their virginity. At every turn and twist, our kids will be forced to take a stand for their values. If they don't ever see their parents having to take a stand, they will usually feel all alone in their struggles.

I'm certainly not advocating that we go around picking fights, but we can look for ways of modeling what we mean when we tell them not to give in to peer pressure.

For instance, when is the last time you took on a TV program for its lack of decency? Most of us have turned off the set at times, indignant about the antifamily messages. But how much better would it be for our kids to see us taking an active role in trying to change the standards? Better yet, we could get them involved in helping us with a letter-writing campaign to TV advertisers.

Or what about the video store around the corner? Instead of simply steering clear of the adult video section when we go to rent a movie, how much more impact could we make by canceling our membership and letting the management know why?

How about taking some time to work at a soup kitchen, or to collect blankets for a homeless shelter? Have you ever considered joining in a prolife rally or taking a place in the next life-chain in your area?

Kids need to see their parents stand up for what they believe. And when they do, they will be much more likely to take a few stands of their own. More than that, they'll feel good about it when they do.

7. *Reclaim the sabbath.* I don't know when we officially lost the spirit of the sabbath, but I do know we've lost it. I've often found myself looking forward to Mondays, when I can sit back in my office and take a breather.

For many families (ironically, mostly Christian families) Sunday has become the busiest, most stress-filled day of the week. Much of the cause can be traced to churches.

Twice during the same day many of us pack the family into the car to attend services. If you serve on any boards or committees, you have no doubt sacrificed many Sunday afternoons to long meetings. Then there are the many functions that fall under the heading of church activities—potluck dinners, bridal showers, baby showers, ministry meetings—all inevitably scheduled on Sundays.

I think it's time we started reclaiming the sabbath. It's a forgotten biblical mandate—or at the very least a good idea handed down from God.

God speaks about the sabbath in Isaiah:
"If you keep your feet from breaking the Sabbath
and from doing as you please on my holy day,
if you call the Sabbath a delight
and the LORD's holy day honorable,
and if you honor it by not going your own way
and not doing as you please or speaking idle words,
then you will find your joy in the LORD,
and I will cause you to ride on the heights of the land
and to feast on the inheritance of your father Jacob."
The mouth of the LORD has spoken. (Isaiah 58:13-14)
Whatever you believe about our need to keep the sabbath, you will probably agree with me on one point: Nothing would help our relationship with our kids more than finding one day of the week to sit back and enjoy being together. And what better day than the one God has set aside for that purpose?

More than that, what better way to send a clear message to our kids about the importance of God's Word in our lives? If he says we should rest, we should rest!

Making Our Words Count

I hope I've relayed the importance of creating concrete, proactive ways to pass on our spiritual values to our kids. The ideas I've listed are simply that—a few of my ideas. You'll have many of your own. Unless our children see us taking seriously the call to "rise up and be separate," they will see no reason to do the same. If we want them to grow and mature in the Lord, we must model a growing, maturing faith in God.

Otherwise, our words are nothing more than words.

A MESSAGE FOR KID-FRIENDLY MOMS

If I had to list the things that I appreciate most about Ruthie (I'd have to buy more paper), the number one item would read: "She prays for me."

So many times I have turned off my computer late at night and snuggled into bed next to her, only to wake her with my movement. "How is your writing going?" she asks, turning toward me. "It's going well," I answer. "I'm glad," she says, "because I've been praying for you."

I will often come home in rush-hour traffic to find that she and the kids have been on their knees praying for my safety. During our times of prayer together, she never forgets to pray for my business and my writing and my decisions about family and career.

In every area of my life, I can feel the power of God touching me through her prayers. And it has made a wonderful difference in my life—as a husband, father and spiritual leader in my home.

If there is one bit of encouragement I could give to wives regarding the spiritual lives of their husbands, it would be to pray for them. Pray that they will be the kind of father their kids need, the kind of husband you need and the kind of man God needs.

—4—
Image Consultant

*W*HETHER WE REALIZE IT OR NOT, WE FATHERS WILL HAVE A
*greater impact on our children's self-image than any
other force around them. We have more power to damage
or to build their self-esteem than anyone else on earth.*

I liked Billy from the first moment I met him. His quiet, polite
manner seemed refreshing in an age when too few children exhibit
those qualities. His playful grin and large, round-framed glasses made
him look much younger than his age of twelve.

As we walked and visited, I quickly noticed how uncomfortable
Billy was with making eye contact. He never looked directly at me.
Every now and then, he would glance upward in my direction, then
quickly aim his gaze down at the ground in front of him.

"Tell me, Billy, what grade are you in this year?"

"Seventh."

"And what school are you going to?"

"Eagle View."

"Do you enjoy it there?"

"It's okay."

"And what is your favorite subject?"

He thought for a moment. "Math, I guess. I like math."

For a good fifteen minutes our conversation went on much like that. I would ask a question and he would answer it in a word or two. His awkwardness could have easily been interpreted as desire for privacy, but I sensed that he truly enjoyed the attention; he just wasn't used to it. I suspected that he suffered from a poor self-image.

Later, as I sat around the dinner table with his parents and some other adults, I realized the root of Billy's problem: his father, Robert.

"Billy, don't take such big bites!" his father commanded. "Billy, chew with your mouth closed!" "Billy, get your elbows off of the table!" "Billy, you've got food on your teeth!" Over and over. Never once did he include him in the conversation or address him in a positive manner. I tried bringing Billy into the discussion, hoping Robert would take the hint and relax his criticism, but it didn't help.

"Tell me, Billy, do you play any sports?" I asked.

"No, he doesn't," Robert blurted out before Billy had a chance to answer. "I tried to get him to go out for the football team, but he wouldn't do it. He's pretty small for his age, so he probably wouldn't do well at football anyway. He's also too short for basketball. And he says he doesn't like soccer."

He gave out a laugh and patted Billy on the back. "I guess you just weren't meant to play sports, were you, Billy?"

All the while, Billy kept his head down, gazing at the table in front of him.

I found it hard to imagine how a father could be so insensitive. Couldn't he see what he was doing to his son's self-image?

Words That Wound

It's amazing how callous we adults can be when it comes to our children. Without even being aware of it, we often act and speak in ways that would damage even the strongest of egos. So imagine the pain our careless words can inflict on young, vulnerable self-images. With our words we can do irreparable damage.

I consider myself to be a fairly well-rounded, competent person. Those who know me well will say that I have a pretty healthy self-esteem. I'm lucky to have had parents who instilled in me a high sense of self-worth and confidence. Even so, I have some deep insecurities that I expect will plague me until my last days.

Without exception, these self-doubts were caused by careless and hurtful words.

Sometime around the seventh grade, I remember vividly being teased by a group of children about the size of my neck and arms. I was rather tall and lanky at the time, with thin arms and a long, skinny neck. They made up little poems—using every imaginable word that rhymed with *giraffe*—to describe my appearance. It became a running joke with this small, cruel group of kids for the better part of a year. As a result, I did everything I could to try and hide my neck and arms. I started wearing long-sleeved shirts, even in the summer, and wouldn't dream of donning another crew-necked T-shirt in public.

If you could see me today, you'd find this hard to believe. These days, I'm a rather large man, and you'd be hard-pressed to describe me as skinny. I have a great deal of trouble finding shirts that fit off the rack, due mostly to the large size of my neck and arms. Even so, I still find myself wearing clothes that hide my neck and arms.

Intellectually, I know that these insecurities are unfounded. But emotionally, the scars remain. And they still affect the way I think and behave.

Phil, a good friend of mine, appears to radiate self-confidence. He is the life of every party, and can liven up any conversation. It has always amazed me to see how well he can work a crowd until everyone is laughing and joking with him. He's the last person you would ever believe to be struggling with low self-esteem.

But once, Phil confided to me that deep inside he is really an insecure person. "I never quite feel that people really like me," he said.

"I know how to make people laugh, and I know they like my jokes. But I don't think they like *me*."

He went on to explain that he feels ashamed of his appearance. He considers his face too thin and his hips much too small. "My father used to tease me about it a lot," he said. "He'd joke that I had nothing in the back to keep my pants from falling off. He would introduce me as 'my son, the bean-pole.' I don't think he ever understood how much that hurt me."

I thought Phil was a nice-looking man. And I knew people really did like him for who he was, not just for his jokes. It pained me to think that his insecurities kept him from knowing and accepting that fact.

The Need for a Father's Acceptance

There is nothing on earth quite as fragile as a child's self-image. And there is nothing more painful to a child than having his self-image wounded. Imagine, then, how a child feels when his self-image is attacked by one of the two people in his life that he trusts for unconditional love, acceptance and protection.

Ten Phrases Guaranteed to Lower Your Child's Self-Esteem

1. Why can't you be like your sister [brother]?

2. Can't you do anything right?

3. Here, let me do that for you!

4. Can't you stay out of the way?

5. What's the matter with you?

6. I'm not up to dealing with you today!

7. Haven't you finished yet?

8. What have I done to deserve this from you?

9. I wish I had never had kids!

10. Sometimes I feel like just leaving!

Phil's father, I'm certain, loved his son and had good intentions. But through his carelessness, he caused irreparable harm to his son's self-image—harm that his son must now live and deal with.

In his book *Raising Confident Kids*, Robert Barnes Jr. talks of the importance a family plays in molding a healthy self-image in children:

God created us with a need to belong, and it is through belonging to a family that each member—son, daughter, mother, and father—

nurtures his or her self-esteem. . . . God created the family to offer, as no other group on earth could, unconditional love to each of its members. In the family, each member sees value in the other members—value for who they are rather than for what they can do.[1]

A father's arms must be a safe haven from harm for children. Kids are going to be teased and criticized at every turn in their life. Their peers will make fun of them. Their teachers will usually treat them with relative indifference—just one out of twenty students in a class. Their coaches will indirectly teach them that their worth depends on their performance. So where are they going to get the individual love and acceptance they desperately need? If they don't find it at home, they likely won't find it at all.

The Difference a Dad Can Make

Whether we realize it or not, we fathers will have a greater impact on our children's self-image than any other force around them. Though many believe that children look primarily to their mothers for love and acceptance, studies conducted by Josh McDowell and Norm Wakefield have shown that in many cases it is the father who will have the greatest impact on their future and their view of themselves.

In their book *The Dad Difference,* they explain that children often give greater significance to a relationship with their father because he is usually unavailable to them during the day. After conducting numerous surveys, they found that the five most important factors in the formation of a child's self-image are (1) a close relationship with the father, (2) spending a lot of time with the father, (3) spending a lot of time with the mother, (4) feeling secure and loved at home and (5) a grade average of A or B.[2]

Sobering, isn't it? Whether we deserve it or not, our children will be looking to us as the most important, most significant person in their lives. How we treat them, act around them and speak to them will have a greater bearing on their self-image than anything else. We have more power to damage or to build their self-esteem than anyone else on earth.

Top Ten Self-Esteem Builders in Children

Those facts raise an important question. How do we fathers start living up to the mandate we've been given?

Let me share what I consider to be the top ten self-esteem builders in children.

1. *Teach your children to know and love God.* Nothing you can do for your children will instill in them a greater sense of worth and happiness than teaching them to know and love God. Robert Barnes puts it this way:

> Ultimately, God wants us to base our self-esteem on the truth that he is the Father and each of us is a prodigal son or daughter. The fact that the King of creation found me so valuable that he paid for my life with the life of his Son should have a profound impact on my feeling of worth and self-esteem.[3]

Knowing God, and knowing that he cares deeply for each of us, will instill in us a greater sense of individual worth and self-acceptance than anything else. You can do no better than to help your children understand and appreciate God's wonderful, abundant love.

2. *Give your kids "quantity" time.* Some things can't be said often enough. And I can't say enough that fathers need to spend time with their kids. When all is said and done, you can't have a positive impact on your kids' lives unless you are there for them—physically as well as emotionally. No to-do list is as important as your kids. So be prepared to let your social life and hobbies suffer, but not your children.

3. *Give your kids unconditional acceptance, even when they fail.* Every one of us would say without hesitation that we accept our children unconditionally, regardless of how often or how badly they fail. But do we really communicate that acceptance to our kids? Do they really believe we do? It's not enough for *us* to know that we accept

them unconditionally; we also need to be sure *they* know we do.

Several days ago, Ruthie took David to the ice-skating rink to give him some pointers. David and I attend ice-skating classes every Friday, and though he is learning quickly, Ruthie was trying to teach him how to relax and let the skates do the work. After a short while, he stopped on the ice and looked up at her, discouraged. "I'm just not very good at skating, Mom," he said.

Ruthie told me later that she didn't realize the message she had been giving David through her coaching. Though she focused only on his technique, he took the instruction as personal criticism. To him, his acceptance depended on his ability to succeed.

For the rest of the day, Ruthie worked double-time to build up David. I listened to her tell him how proud she was of him and how much she loved having him as a son. If David had doubted his mother's acceptance that afternoon, he certainly didn't feel it by bedtime.

Not a one of us wants our acceptance by others to be based on performance. That goes tenfold for children.

4. *Develop a positive tone and attitude.* Yesterday as I was sitting in my truck making a few notes to myself, I noticed a mother and son walking toward their car just a few feet in front of me. The mother had a scowl on her face, and her young son looked as angry and upset as she did. He muttered that he didn't want to go home, and she mumbled back that she'd be glad to leave him right there in the parking lot if that was what he wanted. They both got into the car, slammed their doors simultaneously and drove away.

Now there's a fun family, I thought to myself. It wasn't hard to see why the boy didn't want to go home. From what I saw, I wouldn't want to either.

If home isn't a fun, positive place to be, then your kids won't want to be there. If a father isn't a happy, positive person, the kids won't want to be around him. Nobody will. And worse, your kids will pick up on the negativism, and no one will want to be around them either.

5. *Give your kids physical affection.* My parents were "hugging

nuts." They hugged us, hugged each other, hugged our friends, hugged strangers, hugged the dogs, hugged the mailman. They hugged anything that moved, and some things that didn't. I truly loved it.

Ruthie and I are a lot like them. We love hugging our children. And they're going to have to get used to it, because we don't intend to stop.

Physical affection toward our children is more than a luxury—it's a necessity. Without it, they will never develop the healthy self-esteem we all want for them.

6. *Make eye contact with your kids.* Several weeks ago our family ate lunch with a few other families at a friend's house. While there, I met Jeff, a physician and one of the young fathers in our church. About halfway through lunch he was paged to come in early for work. Before he left, I noticed him saying goodby to his family. He walked over to his kids, one by one, bent down in front of them and looked them directly in the eyes before kissing them on the cheek and whispering something in their ear. He then did the same for his wife. It was remarkable to watch the look of adoration on the faces of Jeff's family

---

If your job takes you away from home overnight on occasion, try these ideas to help enhance your children's self-esteem.

■ *The night before you leave on a business trip, organize a treasure hunt for the kids. The "treasure" doesn't have to be something material, but it could be a personalized letter that shares your love for them.*

■ *Call home every day. The phone calls don't have to be long, especially if you really can't afford them. But it's a great way to help your family stay connected with you while you're gone.*

■ *Do something special with each child before you leave for the trip. Don't try promising a special outing upon your return. Those things seldom work out.*

■ *If your trip is a long one, send postcards or letters each day. Some dads even mail their kids a card before they leave so they'll have something in the mailbox the first day Dad's gone.*

■ *Cancel or shorten a few business trips (if possible) and use the time to spend with your kids. Just see how their little eyes and hearts open up to you when you tell them why you did it!*

—*adapted from* Daddy's Home, *by Greg Johnson & Mike Yorkey (Wheaton, Ill.: Tyndale House, 1992), pp. 58-59.*

as they watched him leave. They truly loved and admired him, and it was easy to see why.

It is the little gestures that kids notice and appreciate the most: a tender touch, a look in the eye, a kiss on the cheek, a whisper in the ear. These simple yet profound actions capture a child's heart and mind.

7. *Be gentle and tender with your kids.* Yesterday morning I woke up to the best feeling I've had in a long time. As I turned to look at the clock, I felt a small arm wrapped around my waist and a warm body up against my back. Sometime in the early morning hours, David had crawled into bed between Ruthie and me. My movement woke him, and he sat up and smiled.

"Hi, Daddy. How was your night?" he said quietly.

"I had a good night's sleep," I answered. "What about you?"

He grinned from ear to ear. "I woke up and came to sleep with you and Mommy."

For a moment, I thought about explaining to him that he needs to stay in his own bed when he wakes up in the night. He knew the rules of the house. But then I thought, *How important is that right now? How can I possibly ruin a good morning like this by giving him a lecture?* So instead we all went into his sister Kandilyn's room, and the four of us played and snuggled together.

Sometimes we get so caught up in making sure that our children understand our rules and regulations that we forget to be good, loving fathers. We forget to sit back and let a tender moment be tender.

I'm not always that smart or gentle or insightful or flexible, but yesterday morning I was. And last night my son wanted to snuggle again before bedtime, "just like we did this morning." Fatherhood doesn't get any better than that.

8. *Listen to your kids.* This is the self-esteem builder that I most need to work on. I often joke that I have a "low threshold of chaos"—that is, when things around me get loud and hectic, I tend to tune out. And with two kids in the house, things are usually loud and hectic. I'm

sure my kids get blank stares too often when they try to get my attention, but I'm working on it.

Fathers need to listen to their kids. Not just pretend to listen, but *really* listen.

9. *Share in your child's interests.* Several years ago, while visiting my brother, Walter, I went to his son's Little League game. Scott has more interests and activities than any kid I know. He also has a healthy dose of self-esteem. I often say that Scott should be the "Self-Esteem Poster Child." Thanks to his parents, he knows his value as a person.

As I watched the game, I could see that Scott wasn't the best player on his team. He was good, but others were bigger and better. It didn't bother him for a moment, however. He played his heart out just the same. And when he dropped the ball or grounded out, he didn't dwell on it; he went right on trying.

That is typical of Scott. Much of his good attitude and self-esteem can be attributed to his parents and their willingness to share his interests. They wouldn't miss one of his games for anything, and he knows it.

Nothing communicates love and builds our children's self-esteem like our interest and involvement in their lives. Their whole world often revolves around whether they get the next hit, or whether they remember their lines in the school play, or whether they'll be able to reach the high note in front of "all those people" in the auditorium. If we're not there for them during those times, we are sending them the message that their world isn't important to us—that *they* aren't important to us.

10. *Learn to value yourself.* Most of us know that we can't teach what we don't know. And we can't pass on to our children what we don't have.

The way we feel about ourselves affects every area of our behavior—how we dress, act and speak, how we spend our time and money, and especially how we treat our kids. If we don't respect ourselves, we will neither respect our children nor teach them to respect themselves. And on top of it, they won't respect us.

Our children pick up on how we feel about ourselves, and unconsciously they take on many of the same traits and feelings. Unless we value ourselves in a healthy way, we'll have little chance of instilling a sense of self-worth in our children.

Raising People-Friendly Kids

To do justice to the subject of self-esteem is beyond the scope of this book. Here I've simply tried to encourage fathers to view themselves and their children as valuable, precious, worthwhile people.

Our children will be actively looking to the world around them for a sense of who they are and how they fit into the grand scheme of things. And how they come to feel about themselves depends upon how they sense others feel about them.

The question we must ask is, "Are we willing to let their peers, teachers, friends, coworkers, and every stranger they meet set the tone for their future? Or are we going to reserve that job for ourselves?"

The answer is obvious: I want to be the brightest guiding light in their lives. And I want them to feel about themselves the way *I* feel about them, and the way I know that God feels about them, not the way others might happen to see them.

More than that, I want to instill in them the kind of heart that is sensitive to the feelings and needs of others—the kind of heart that Christ expects of Christians. Only when a child feels good about his value as a person will he be able to sense the needs of others. Only when they respect and love themselves will they be free to give others the respect and love that Christ wants us to give.

Not so long ago, David and I were driving home from the grocery store when he abruptly turned to me and smiled widely. "So, Daddy," he began in his most adult voice, "Mommy told me that the people want to publish one of your books."

I glanced over at him and smiled back. "That's right, they do. Isn't that exciting?"

"Yeah, isn't that exciting?" Just then, I felt his tiny hand patting me on the back. "I'm so proud of you," he said, still smiling and looking up at me. "You're such a good Daddy. I'm so proud of my good Daddy."

There is no joy on earth like that of watching your children grow up to be sweet, happy and caring people. To see them grow in love and compassion for others. To watch their hearts and minds open to the world around them.

But only a kid-friendly dad can hope to instill those qualities in his children. Their sense of self—as well as their future—hinges on our willingness to live the kind of lives we want them to have. One of the highest goals of every kid-friendly dad should be to see that his children become compassionate, Christian people.

That's when we'll know that we're doing something right.

A MESSAGE FOR KID-FRIENDLY MOMS

I've noticed that the times when I naturally encourage others are those times when I am feeling good about myself. When my self-esteem is at a high point, I am more able and willing to reach out to others who might be feeling a little low.

Most feelings and emotions are like that. When we are happy, we usually brighten up the day for others. When we are sad, we bring others down. When we are depressed, those around us start feeling blue and melancholy as well. That's especially true in our families. A father's mood and temperament often set the tone for everyone.

A wife can do much to help steer her husband toward setting a positive tone in the family. Her reactions toward him can make a big difference in how he feels about himself and about his role as a father.

Ruthie does wonders for my self-image through the small things she says and does. She lets me know how much she appreciates me as a husband and as a father. She tells me often how proud she is of me and my accomplishments.

Men need to know that they are respected and appreciated by their wives. And they need to know that their efforts in making a living are not going unnoticed.

When a husband's self-image is what it should be, he is much more likely to pay attention to the needs and feelings of his wife and children. Not only will he be happier and more content, but he'll also be a better husband and father.

— 5 —
Financial
Adviser

*T*O LIVE A SIMPLE, HONEST LIFE. TO STAY OUT OF DEBT. TO
*give regularly and readily. To hold our possessions lightly.
To be content with what we have. These are strange concepts
in the eyes of society. But they are ones that God demands—both from
us and our children.*

Let's call him Tommy—an average American child in a typical
family. His father works, and perhaps his mother works part-time.
They're not rich, but they live comfortably, seldom wanting for the
essentials of life.

As Tommy grows up, he learns quickly what is and isn't important
in the lives of his parents. At mealtimes, much of the conversation
revolves around material things. During breakfast, Dad reads about
the new tax laws being proposed by Congress and wonders aloud what
effect it will have on his income. At dinner, brother Bobby begs his
parents for a new pair of $150 Nike sneakers; but sister Sally objects,
insisting that she first be allowed to buy the $90 Guess jeans that she
desperately "needs."

Mom firmly reminds them to wait their turn. "I've just ordered new drapes, you know. And we have to pay off the credit cards before we can shop for more clothes."

Through the years, Tommy sees his parents go more and more upscale with each promotion. They move into a nicer house, even though the last one seemed nice enough to Tommy. And a few years later, another promotion comes and once again the family is house-hunting—not for a bigger house, but for a better neighborhood.

One day he sees Dad leave the house in their two-year-old Pontiac Bonneville and come home a few hours later with a new Lexus. The old car seemed fine to Tommy. But since Dad sometimes entertains business clients at lunch, he felt it was important to make a good impression.

During Tommy's junior year in high school, he begins to think about college, and he and Dad sit down in the living room to go over some of the catalogs they've ordered. The discussion starts out on a practical level. How far away from home will he be? Will he live in the dorm or off-campus? What scholarships might be available at the different universities?

But soon they get down to the important issues. What school will look best on a résumé? Which schools are the big companies looking to for young employees? And which careers will give him the most earning potential?

Tommy goes to college and works harder than usual on his grades at the prodding of his father. "A good GPA is essential in today's job market," he tells Tommy over the phone. "If you want a good-paying job, you have to have good grades. It's as simple as that."

After graduating, Tommy finds a good job, marries his college sweetheart and buys a nice starter-home—more than they can really afford, but one that they hope their budget will grow into.

Tommy has learned from his childhood how life works. Money dominates every major decision. He'll spend his life always looking forward to the next promotion, a better-paying job, a bigger house, a better neighborhood, a nicer car. He will always judge himself and others by income and social status. For Tommy, net worth will always be the bottom line.

The Vicious Cycle

Our worlds often revolve around money or the lack of it. Where we live, how we act, how we dress, who we associate with, where we go on vacation, what kinds of cars we drive—all these and more depend directly on how much money we make. These are society's standards of success, the criteria by which others will judge us. And how others view us directly affects the way we view ourselves. It's part of human nature to want to be liked and to feel good about ourselves, and money is a means to that end.

Christ, however, calls us to be different. He calls us to view ourselves and others in a different light. While the world screams at us to get to the top, Christ gently beckons us to humble ourselves as servants. While society speaks of a dog-eat-dog world, where in order to survive we must "look out for number one," Christ tells us to love our enemies and pray for those who put us down.

The mandate from Scripture is clear: we are called to be different, to pursue lives of service and to reach for treasures far better than those of the world.

Luxury or Christian Service?

From my days in college, I remember well two different posters hanging in dormitory rooms around the campus. Their messages were worlds apart.

One poster had a photo of a jet-black Rolls Royce parked in the driveway of a large, opulent mansion. In front of the car stood a woman in exquisite formal wear lifting a champagne glass. The inscription read, "My tastes are simple. I want the best of everything."

The other poster was a picture of a bum in a dark alley, slouched against the curb, his clothes torn and dirty. He held a bottle in a paper bag, and he was surrounded by filth and debris. The inscription? "You love Jesus only as much as the person you love the least."

I've always been struck by the stark contrast between these two posters. One tells us that the road to happiness is paved with wealth and materialism. The other calls us to set aside our personal happiness and look to the needs of others.

As Christians, we have to decide which slogan we will make our own. Which of these two posters will hang on the walls of our hearts?

As fathers, we have another question to deal with. Which of these slogans do we want to see our children nail on *their* heartwalls? Which view of the world will they hold as their own?

> *"That's the trouble with trying to run in the rat race. Even if you win, you're still a rat."*
>
> —Lily Tomlin

Bigger Is Better?

Not long ago, I was visiting with David in his room, and out of the blue he exclaimed, "We need a bigger house."

His statement took me by surprise. "Why is that?" I asked him.

"Because my room is too small. I need a bigger room for all my toys."

I didn't think much of the conversation at the time, but later that night while reflecting back on it, I became concerned. Though our house is no mansion, it certainly isn't small. The house I grew up in was much smaller, and my parents had five children while we only have two. I don't remember ever thinking of my parents' house as being small. In fact, it seemed huge to me. What would make David dissatisfied with our house?

Soon the answer hit me. He was merely imitating his parents.

At the time, Ruthie and I had been shopping for a larger house. Our reasons were quite practical. I keep an office in the house, and our family has grown over the last few years, so we really could use the extra room. Also, interest rates were at an all-time low, and the real estate market was prime for a good buy on a larger home. From a financial standpoint, it was a good time to move. But that's not the message we were giving to our kids.

If you've ever been house shopping, you know how it affects your attitude. Something happens after you spend a few days walking through large, well-designed homes, only to come home later to your own familiar, drab place again. It can make you terribly dissatisfied.

Ruthie and I soon found ourselves complaining daily about all the things we didn't like about our present home. The bathrooms started to look smaller, the kitchen suddenly had too little cabinet space, and my office became more cramped by the day. Soon we began to wonder how we ever could have bought such a small, simple house in the first place.

We also began to raise our standards for the new home. With every house we viewed, our wish-list grew. I soon decided I couldn't live without a large deck in the yard. Ruthie wanted a large master suite with a private bath. We both wanted an oversized den and a formal dining room.

The strangest thing about this escapade is that Ruthie and I are not especially materialistic. We're usually quite content with what we have. But we found ourselves being easily dragged into a pit of greed. And worse, we saw our children following suit.

For now, we've decided to put our moving plans on hold. We're not ruling out finding a larger home in the future, but we are committed to having our priorities in the right order when we do. We plan to let God play a much larger role in the decision next time. And we'll be satisfied with whatever house he leads us to.

The Greed Monster
Greed is a strange animal. It can pull you in faster and easier than almost any other vice on earth. No subject in Scripture is addressed more often—or condemned more readily—than the love of money.

As fathers, we will do well to help our children steer clear of this all-consuming monster. To model freedom from materialism should be at the top of our agenda. Otherwise our children, like Tommy, will believe that self-worth and success depend on the number of zeros at the end of their paycheck.

It would break my heart to see my children become enslaved by materialism and begin to measure their worth by their net worth. To a large degree, it's up to me to keep that from happening. Once again, the key to their future begins with me. How I view money—the importance it plays in my life—will most likely determine how they will view money. That means I must be willing to ask myself some tough and important questions while they're still young. If I expect my kids to have their financial priorities in order, I must first see that my own are.

Financial Issues for Fathers

1. *Am I a good steward?* God calls us to be good stewards of our time and money. Most of us are familiar with the parable of the talents in

---

Four Steps to Combat Materialism

1. Simplify your lifestyle. Most of us think we're a victim to the high cost of living, when we're really victims to the cost of living high. If you live above your means, learn to downsize your lifestyle.

2. Think before you buy. Before making any purchases, we should ask ourselves five questions: (a) Is this a purchase of need or greed? (b) Have I fulfilled all of my other financial obligations? (c) Will this purchase affect my ability to give God what I've committed to give? (d) Have I prayed about this purchase? (e) Have I shopped around to see that I'm getting the best deal for my money? If we honestly face these questions, most of our purchasing decisions will be sound.

3. Pray for contentment. Paul wrote in his letter to the Philippians (4:12) about the joy that comes through contentment. Dissatisfaction with the things we have will always cause us to want more. If we truly want to be free from materialism, we must pray for contentment.

4. Relinquish control of your material goods. When we truly turn our lives over to God—when we relinquish control of our earthly wants and wishes—we will find ourselves free from the bonds of materialism.

Matthew 25. Though the story primarily addresses the issue of winning lost souls, it has a much broader application. How we use what we have is important to God—our time, gifts, talents, money or the ability to make money.

As a father, I need to take a long, hard look at my "portfolio of talents." Am I doing the best I can with what God has given me? Am I investing wisely in the future—both mine and my family's? Am I gaining the best interest I can on the earthly holdings God has entrusted to me?

I don't want to end up like the poor steward in the parable. Nor do I want my kids to.

2. *Am I giving back to God what is God's?* Many Christians debate about whether we are called to tithe. "That's an Old Testament thing," some say. "We're New Testament Christians, and we're no longer under the old law."

Weak argument. The Israelites in the Old Testament were called to give ten percent; Jesus' followers—and Christians today—are called to give one hundred percent. If anything, a tithe is inadequate.

The best advice you can give your kids about money is to tell them to tithe. And they will listen to you only if they know you've held yourself to the same standard.

3. *Am I staying out of debt?* Proverbs 22:7 says, "The borrower is servant to the lender." We all know how true that is. If you've ever bought a new car, you've also received a payment book as thick as a dictionary. And if you think you're not a slave to this book, try missing a few payments and see how long it takes for your master to come looking for you!

Nothing has led more good, decent people into the throes of financial bondage than easy payment plans and long lines of credit. "Buy now, pay later" has become a way of life. We simply can't keep up with the Joneses without it.

There is only one way out of the vicious cycle of debt. We must choose not to participate. We must decide to let the Joneses be the

Joneses, and wave goodbye as they climb ahead of us on the material ladder. If we want to remain free from bondage—as well as make a strong, clear statement to our children about our true priorities—we must commit as much as possible to "paying as we go."

On a practical level, this may call for some tough decisions regarding our purchasing habits. Buying on credit may be convenient, but is it the most responsible use of our resources? How much more could be done with our money if we disciplined ourselves to save and *make* interest on our money instead of paying it?

Several years ago, Ruthie and I decided to cut up our credit cards. It was a very tough decision, but it has proved to be the best financial move we've made. It's amazing how much further our monthly paycheck goes when so little of it is obligated to creditors.

Few of us are able to buy a house or a car without borrowing, but if we limit our debt to those few, large purchases, our lives (and wallets) will be much less stressed.

4. *Am I financially honest?* In 1991, a nationwide study uncovered some sad news about honesty in America. Over 91 percent of the population admit to being dishonest on a regular basis. Over half of that number said they couldn't get through a week without lying about something to someone. Sadder still, 31 percent did not believe that "honesty is the best policy."[1]

Personal integrity has taken quite a nosedive over the last few decades—especially, I suspect, in the area of finances. Dishonesty reigns when it comes to money.

We need to be clear exceptions to that rule. Not just in order to be good fathers, but in order to be good Christians.

Someone once joked that every man keeps three sets of books—one to show his banker, one to show the IRS, and one to show what he really makes. Judging from the above survey, that may not be far from wrong. But if we're serious about modeling financial values to our kids, we need to see that our own money is managed honestly and wisely.

5. *Do I hold material possessions with a loose hand?* It has always

struck me as hypocritical when we parents force our children to share their toys with other kids while many of us wouldn't dream of sharing some of our "toys" with our neighbors. We all know how hard it is to relinquish our car keys to a friend in need, or loan our power saw to the next-door neighbor. And yet we expect our kids to share without hesitation.

Noted speaker Bill Gothard often tells the story of his first car. He was so proud of it that he spent half of his time washing, waxing and admiring it. It was his prize possession. One day a woman slammed into him, wrecking the car beyond repair. The loss devastated him. He agonized over the wreck, wondering over and over why it had happened and how he could ever afford to replace such a fine automobile.

Then one night it occurred to him that the day he became a Christian he had pledged to relinquish total control of his life to God—including his earthly possessions. Right then and there he renewed his vow to the Lord.

After that, a heavy burden was lifted from his shoulders. "It was no longer *my* car that had been wrecked—it was God's. And if God wanted to wreck his car, who was I to say that he shouldn't?"

He goes on to add that if God wanted to replace the car, he would. "It was in God's hands to worry about, not mine."

Teaching our children to be nonmaterialistic must start with an open hand on our part. If we love our things too much to share them with others, they will learn to do the same.

6. *Am I content with what I have?* Paul talked about contentment in his letter to the Philippians:

I know what it is to be in need, and I know what it is to have plenty. I have learned the secret of being content in any and every situation, whether well fed or hungry, whether living in plenty or in want. (Philippians 4:12)

The writer of Hebrews also warned against greed and discontentment:

Keep your lives free from the love of money and be content with what you have. (Hebrews 13:5)

Nothing will create a materialistic heart faster than an attitude of discontentment. Dissatisfaction with the things we have will always cause us to want more. That kind of home atmosphere becomes a breeding ground for greedy, materialistic kids.

A Tough Calling for the Nineties

As Christians, we are called to go against the grain of society's habits and expectations by holding ourselves to a biblical view of money. We are called to live a simple, honest life. To stay out of debt. To give regularly and readily. To hold our possessions lightly. To be content with what we have. These are strange concepts in the eyes of society. But they are ones that God demands—from us and our children.

As kid-friendly dads, we have our work cut out for us in this area. It's a tough calling to live up to, but it's an important one. Our children need to understand what it means to serve only one master. And as their financial advisers, we'll have to practice what we preach.

Let's not drop the ball when the stakes run this high.

A MESSAGE FOR KID-FRIENDLY MOMS

Men today face enormous pressure to be financially successful. At work, at church, at social gatherings, on the golf course with friends, we feel we are being sized up and categorized based on the make of our car, the status of our neighborhood and the thickness of our financial portfolio. Keeping our materialistic tendencies under control is not always easy—especially when so many place such a high priority on earthly possessions.

The last thing a dad needs is to feel that his wife isn't pleased with the standard of living that he is able to provide—that she too, in subtle ways, bases his worth on his net worth.

When I find myself feeling the pressure to work harder and bring home more money—pressure generated from myself, my friends and business associates—Ruthie has a way of helping me bring my priorities back in order. She reminds me that we have much more than we'll ever need, and that our ultimate goal is to raise happy, healthy children, not to build bigger and better houses to impress our friends.

A wife who is truly content with what she has will help relieve a lot of pressure from an already overstressed, heavily burdened husband.

— 6 —
Career Guidance Counselor

*U*LTIMATELY, A FATHER'S ROLE IN GUIDING HIS CHILDREN *into their chosen careers is to see that they have all the facts they need to make a good decision; to make sure that they are the kind of men and women who will make right choices; and to see that their relationship with God is such that they will look to him more than they look to us.*

Had I listened to my high-school guidance counselor, today I would probably be crammed in a cubicle, crunching numbers for a large corporation. Had I taken the advice of my seventh-grade football coach, I might be carrying an extra fifty pounds of muscle, chasing a quarterback around the field every weekend. Had my fate been in the hands of my eighth-grade science teacher, I would probably be sweeping up after parades.

These are all noble and needed professions, but they're not me. I'd be miserable doing any of those things. None of them represent my interests or—as far as I know—my talents.

Today I'm doing what I love. My time is divided between running a small-but-growing business and writing. No one thought I would be able to make a living at either one, much less be successful—except my parents. They knew I could excel at anything I wanted to do—or so they had me believe. Even so, the odds and the facts were against me.

As a young boy I was shy, inarticulate, terrible with numbers and seemingly unmotivated. I was anything but a leader. No one then ever imagined that I could effectively run a company. When it came to business, I had little in my favor besides a burning ambition. And yet over the years I have owned and managed several successful businesses, including the one I now oversee.

Writing, my first love and second career, is a profession that should have chewed me up and spit me out long ago. No English teacher in my past—with one exception—would have ever visualized my name on the cover of a book or the byline of an article. My grammar was "appalling," my punctuation "unacceptable" and my misspelling frequent. Sentence structure, I am told, was my only strong suit, which at best made my essays decipherable. For all practical purposes, typing class should have been my biggest waste of time. But it has proved to be the most productive "easy-A" class I've ever taken.

At any rate, today I make a living doing the two things that should have never provided me with a livable paycheck. Nothing about my career was predictable at an early age.

The same is probably true for our children. As fathers, we should never underestimate or overestimate the career potential of our children. In fact, the worst thing we can possibly do is to try to set their goals and ambitions for them. That's *their* job. Our job is to broaden their horizons, encourage them, keep them motivated and on track, and watch them from an accessible distance as they find their own professional direction.

It's a frightening thing to do. It's unnatural not to want to push our children into a career that we feel is ripe for them. We see their talents. We see their shortcomings. We see them heading toward success or failure long before they do. It's only right that we should want to intervene. But it would be a mistake. No, it would be a travesty. It would mean becoming the proverbial stage mother to the shy, unwilling ballerina. We all know how pathetic that can be.

As a young man, my father-in-law, Bob, had a gift for playing the piano. He was a rare talent, with nimble fingers and a keen ear for music. A rich aunt saw this talent and began cultivating it. By the time he was ready to leave for college, his future had already been planned for him. He was to attend an elite school of music and become a concert pianist.

At about this time, he announced one day that he would be going to a Christian college to study Bible. Despite his aunt's wishes, he felt strongly that his calling was to become a minister. His aunt was livid, and she threatened to cut him out of her inheritance if he didn't change his mind. He didn't.

That was forty-five years ago. Today, Bob is still ministering to those in need, and his service to the Lord has touched lives on many continents around the world. I couldn't begin to count the number of lives that have been brought to Christ because of his decision to shun the demands of his aunt and follow his true calling instead.

A Matter of Trust

I strongly believe that the best career advice we can give our kids is to encourage them to trust God and to trust their instincts. If we help them carry nothing into adulthood other than a deep trust in God the Father and a strong belief in themselves, we will have done them justice.

I mentioned earlier that there was one teacher in my past who was an exception to the rest. It was my tenth-grade American literature teacher, Mrs. Jackson. Whether she saw in me the next great Hemingway or simply a shy, pimple-faced kid who needed encouragement, I'll never know. But she made me believe in myself as a writer. Under her guidance, I tried harder, worked more, and wrote better than I ever had in my life.

While other teachers were splashing red ink all over every page I wrote, she was reading aloud to the class what I had written, praising the "vivid imagery" and "captivating characters." I know now that most of it was pitiful stuff. But at the time, I truly felt that I would one day write the great American novel.

She taught me to believe in myself.

More than anyone else, Ruthie has taught me to trust in God. Through every turn in our lives, she has helped me see that God's hand is with us. While I often worry about how the business is doing or whether the editors will like my next book idea or how I'm going to meet the next deadline, she reminds me that everything is in God's hands.

Nothing has served me better in my life and my career than these two lessons. And it is these two lessons that I want instilled into the hearts and minds of my children.

Putting Careers in Perspective

A career is something you do; it is not who you are. That's another lesson I want to pass on to my kids. Though God cares deeply about what we do for a living, he cares much, much more about who we are and how we go about doing it. Whether my kids become astronauts, lawyers, doctors, ministers or parking lot sweepers, God will see them in the same light, and so will I.

That is not to say, however, that I don't want my kids to work hard at their careers. As Christians, we have an obligation—a biblical mandate—to be the best we can be at whatever we do:

Go to the ant, you sluggard;
    consider its ways and be wise!
It has no commander,
    no overseer or ruler,
yet it stores its provisions in summer
    and gathers its food at harvest.

How long will you lie there, you sluggard?
When will you get up from your sleep?
A little sleep, a little slumber,
 a little folding of the hands to rest—
and poverty will come on you like a bandit
 and scarcity like an armed man. (Proverbs 6:6-11)

God wants us to succeed at our careers. But he also wants us to keep our careers and goals in perspective. I like the way Jerry Jenkins, editor of *Moody* magazine, describes his career goals:

> The goal I have set for myself as a writer is one that must always be striven for and is much more easily measured than the other. I want to be the best writer I can be. If that still places me one hundredth or one thousandth on the list, so be it. It is an achievable goal, and I pray my motive is right. What if I were first on the list and still not the best I could be? That would be tragic, a waste, and not an acceptable offering to God.[1]

Our goal should be to do the best we can at whatever we do. And we should see that our children learn that lesson as well.

More on Goal-Setting

Goals are wonderful things to have. Most of us would be nowhere without them. Businesses that operate without goals are usually left in the dust by their competitors. Churches without goals usually go nowhere, eventually focusing inward and maintaining the status quo instead of helping and serving and growing. People without goals often die having accomplished few of the things they should or could have accomplished. Most successful men will point to their ability to set and carry out goals as the secret behind their success. Goals are wonderful and important things, and I will encourage my kids to set many in their lives.

But just as important as setting goals is knowing what goals we should and shouldn't be setting. Just because we desire to do something doesn't mean it should become our goal. I have a desire to write a bestselling pulp novel the size of *War and Peace,* and I believe I could do it, but that should not be my goal. My wife has a desire to move to Vienna, rent a loft overlooking the river and retire, but that should not be her goal. Goals should have clear, concise purposes behind them. Once accomplished, we should be able to see the benefits. And they should be things that benefit the kingdom of God, not our own personal wants and desires.

I know a man who has a goal to reach every household of Mexico with the message of the gospel. He doesn't assume that this goal is an easy one, or that it will even be accomplished in his lifetime, but he does hope to see it happen. And it has become his life's goal.

> **Setting Goals Worthy of Achieving**
>
> *We fathers should not only teach our kids to set goals but also help them to set goals worthy of achieving. Here are some questions they can ask themselves before setting and carrying out their goals.*
>
> ■ *What is my motivation? Why am I setting this goal? For money? Recognition? Self-improvement? Or is this a goal God wants me to achieve?*
>
> ■ *What is my purpose? Who will be helped if I achieve this goal? Why is this goal worth working toward?*
>
> ■ *What is my strategy? If this is a goal worthy of setting, how do I plan on going about achieving it?*
>
> ■ *What is my time schedule? Goals worth working toward must be planned out on a time schedule. If time schedules are not set, goals usually go unachieved.*

Ruthie and I have a goal to see that our children and their children grow to know and love the Lord—to see that our family circle goes unbroken. It's an important goal, and it's a right goal.

A Father's Role

Ultimately, a father's role in guiding his children into their chosen careers is to see that they have all the facts they need for a good decision; to make sure that they are the kind of men and women who will make right choices; and to see that their relationship with God is such that they will look to him more than they look to us.

The day my children announce that they have decided what they want to do for a living, the temptation will be very strong to sit them down and throw out a string of questions. "Are you sure that's where your talents lie? Do you know how well that job will support you? Have you considered . . . ?"

I hope to fight that temptation. When that day comes, I want to have but one question on my lips: "Have you prayed and studied about this?" All of my concerns should revolve around that thought.

Before that time comes, I hope I will have done my job. If I have exposed them to as many different life experiences and hobbies as possible, instilled in them a strong work ethic, modeled a life of trust in God and belief in myself as a provider, demonstrated a prayer life that includes God in every major decision I make, and tried as much as possible to make right decisions in my life, I will have given them all they need to make their own choices—in their careers and their lives.

The rest is between them and God.

A MESSAGE FOR KID-FRIENDLY MOMS
Albert Schweitzer once wrote, "The only people who will be really happy are those who have sought and found how to serve."[2]

Though we should not push our kids into careers based on what we think they should do, we can and should pray that they ultimately decide to do what Christ would want of them. Whether it be as the head of a major corporation or as the pulpit minister of a small church, we are all called to be servants of Christ in the world.

Mothers have a golden opportunity while their children are young to instill in them a heart for Christian service and a desire to do good deeds for others. Take them to visit someone who is alone; prepare meals for the sick and dependent; help them clean up an elderly person's yard. Teach them to look for needs and then fill them.

A heart for service will affect every future decision they make—especially what they choose to do for a living.

— 7 —
Shop
Teacher

A SHARED INTEREST GIVES OUR CHILDREN TIME TO CATCH VAL-
ues from us. It allows us to talk to them, to interact with them,
to teach them teamwork, to show them the joy of accomplishment and creativity. But more than that, it allows us to get to know our
children.

I stood to one side, watching his eyes closely as he ran his fingers
over the joints of the table in front of him. He leaned forward, carefully
examining the smooth finish. With a hand on either side, he turned it
upside down, running his eyes from one corner to the next, feeling
each joint and nail hole as he went.

"You did a nice job," he said with a smile. "You did a real nice
job."

I was elated. This was the first piece of furniture I had ever built
entirely on my own—a glass-top coffee table. And I'll never forget
the thrill of hearing my father's words of encouragement. Not just
because he was my father, but because he was also a skilled carpenter
who knew good workmanship from bad. He had taught me how to

build, and I really wanted to impress him.

Since then, I've always kept up with woodworking as a hobby. I've built much of the furniture in our house, including the desk I'm sitting at this moment. I've found woodworking to be a tremendous source of stress relief and satisfaction, and it saves money as well. It's a craft I owe to my father's willingness to take me under his wing and teach me. I also hope to introduce it to my children when they grow older.

Bonding Relationships

Woodworking wasn't the only hobby that my father and I shared, but it was the most enjoyable and memorable one. We worked on cars together, but that never really appealed to me. We went fishing together, but neither of us ever developed the knack for bringing in the "big ones." We both enjoyed building, however, and we did it every chance we got.

During those times working by his side, I felt a special bond with my father. I felt close to him. Though I had always known I was part of the family, during these times I felt like an indispensable part. Had I not been there to hold that board in place for Dad, I felt, the cabinet would have never been finished. Had I not been there to help lift the ceiling beams onto the roof, that garage would have never gotten off of the ground floor. I was a part of the process. In my eyes, it couldn't have been done without me.

As we worked together, my father and I also got to know each other. We talked about things that might never have surfaced otherwise. Once, while working in the garage, I learned of the time a wagon filled with logs ran over my father's foot, crushing the nail of his big toe. Right then he took off his shoe to show me. While paneling a back room of the house I heard all about Dad's early days in the cotton fields of Louisiana. I never dreamed how hard that type of work could be.

Working with wood afforded us countless hours of uninterrupted conversation. I cherish those times together. They've been permanently etched into my memory and my heart. And they've taught me a valuable lesson about family togetherness and association.

A Time for Value-Catching

It has been said that values are caught, not taught. A father can talk until he is blue in the face about what his children should believe and how they should think, but unless his own actions back up those beliefs, his words will be lost in the wind. I can warn my kids of the evils of alcohol daily, but if they see me drinking, you can bet the farm that they'll do the same. I can preach a thousand sermons to my kids on the virtues of sacrificial giving, but if I hold my wallet with a tight hand, they'll be tightwads as well.

If we want our kids to catch our values, we must do two things: first, make sure that our values are worth catching, and second, spend enough time with our kids to let those values rub off. That's where hobbies can come in handy. A shared interest gives our children time to catch values from us. It gives us time to talk to our kids, to interact with them, to teach them the value of teamwork, to show them the joy of accomplishment and creativity. But more than that, it allows us to get to know our children, and allows them to get to know us.

Miles, a friend of our family, is a self-proclaimed "hobby nut." Unlike those who dabble in hobbies in their spare time, Miles takes his interests seriously. When he takes up a new hobby (which he does frequently), he throws himself

If you love hobbies but feel guilty about the time they take away from your kids, here's a list of hobbies you and your children can pursue together:

- *Collecting sports cards, stamps, coins*
- *Fishing*
- *Building electric train layouts*
- *Woodworking*
- *Building model cars, planes or rockets*
- *Photography, building and using a darkroom*
- *Gardening*
- *Ice skating, rollerblading, hockey*
- *Repairing cars*
- *Playing computer games*
- *Skiing*
- *Bike riding*
- *Memorizing Scripture*
- *Other_____*

(fill in the blank)

headlong into it. Over the years, his hobbies have included horse-train-
ing, rodeo-riding, deep-sea diving, photography, camping and many
more.

As his list of interests expanded, he would always introduce his
children to the hobby as well. Whatever activity he took up became a
family activity, something they all did together. Today, his children
love and admire him as much as ever. Their faith is strong, their values
are impeccable, and their self-images are healthy and high. They too
have become "hobby-nuts" in their own right, sharing the joy of new
discoveries with their own children.

While many fathers were finding themselves frustrated when their
hobbies took time away from their families, Miles learned instead to
use them to his advantage. He used these varied interests to rally his
family together.

If you, like me, enjoy a nice round of golf on the weekends, but feel
guilty about taking the time away from your kids, why not take your
kids with you? You'll be surprised at how fast you've grown a new
golf partner.

If fishing is your sport, why spend all those precious hours at the
lake by yourself while your kids sit at home in front of the TV? Most
children would be thrilled to spend a day at the lake with Dad, trying
to nab that ten-pounder.

Whatever hobbies or interests you might have, why not use them
as a springboard to get to know your children? You'll be building a
bond that will last a lifetime.

Encouraging Kids to Think

There are other reasons to expose our children to as many different
hobbies and interests as possible. Hobbies tend to foster creativity and
problem-solving ability. They keep children's minds active and their
hands busy. They teach children to think and do for themselves.

A big complaint I have with television is that it fosters dependence
on others for entertainment and leaves creativity to those who produce

the shows. Instead of thinking creatively, kids learn to let their mind flow with whatever they happen to be watching. Plots are developed and problems solved without any thinking on their part. Television forces children to be passive observers in a world of promotion and razzle-dazzle.

I have the same problem with video and computer games. Yes, they require more mental activity than television, but they leave little room for creativity and imagination. Kids need to create, to solve problems, to dream and then to fulfill those dreams.

Author Joe White tells of a dream he had as a young man to design and create a huge fountain along a main street in his hometown. His father, whose business was able to provide him with the materials and equipment, decided to fund his son's dream and send him to work. White writes:

> I didn't do everything right. During one crisis in the field engineering stage, as we poured concrete and worked like crazy as it set up, Daddy sweated and worked shoulder-to-shoulder with me so I wouldn't fail.
>
> Daddy taught me how to dream dreams. He dreamed with me. He helped my dreams come true. The fountain and that sugar maple are monuments not to the kid who built and planted them, but to the daddy who encouraged him along the way. Daddy taught me how to have a vision . . . to create an idea and help that idea mature into full bloom.[1]

When we teach our kids to create a vision and work toward it, we are teaching them not only creativity but also discipline and endurance. We're teaching them to follow through with their plans. And once finished, they can feel good about themselves and what they've achieved. They discover they are capable of accomplishing much more than they realized.

Some years ago I set out to build a slat-back rocking chair. I knew it would be more difficult than anything I had previously built, but I was determined to try. After a few days in the workshop, I realized the

project was taking much more time and planning than I had antici-
pated. The first few tries didn't work. The braces weren't holding up,
and the legs were collapsing underneath me when I sat down. The
problem wasn't in the building, but in the designing and engineering.
I wasn't sure I'd be able to do it. But my dad came to my rescue and
worked by my side until the job was finished.

Today that rocker sits proudly in the family room of our house. It
is far from the best-looking piece of furniture I've built, but it is the
one that I am the most proud of.

Paving the Way to a Career

Another byproduct of introducing kids to a variety of hobbies is that
we may help lead them toward a future profession. We all know people
who have turned hobbies into successful businesses or careers; it could
happen with our own children.

For example, writing was nothing more than a hobby to me for
years. I spent many an afternoon in my youth writing short stories and
essays, none of which were ever intended for publication. I'd finish
them and file them away. It didn't occur to me that I was honing my
skills for a future career; I just enjoyed writing as a hobby. It relaxed
me. Years later, this hobby turned into a second profession.

A good friend of mine grew up with an interest in building and
programming small computers. This was long before the days of
personal computing, when the only computers around were large
mainframes in schools and businesses. But it was possible to order
parts from the back of magazines and build one's own "computer" at
home. In those days they were more like glorified calculators than
computers, but my friend enjoyed doing it in his spare time.

He finished college with a degree in chemistry, assuming he'd be
working in a laboratory the rest of his life. But today he is a key
employee for a large computer corporation, where he helps design and
build the world's fastest, most advanced computers. "I don't know
that I could even find my diploma today," he recently remarked. "But

that doesn't matter, because what I do has nothing to do with chemistry."

In spite of his many years in school, it was his hobby that helped pave the way to a successful, rewarding career.

Nobody Loses with Hobbies

Ruthie and I often sit and wonder aloud what our children will be doing twenty, thirty or forty years from now. When David and I spend an evening at the pool, I wonder if he'll want to be a world-class diver someday. When we attend our weekly ice-skating classes, I envision him as a professional hockey player, leading the league in scores. When I see him bowing his head in prayer, I wonder if he will someday fill a church pulpit, giving his life to the full-time work of the Lord.

When I watch Kandilyn caring for her dolls, making them little beds in her crib and then covering them from the cold, I wonder if she'll one day become a nurse or a doctor or a wonderful, caring mother.

Whatever my kids decide to do, I hope they do it because they enjoy it and because they feel a calling to do it, not because they feel unqualified to do anything else. That would be sad, and it would be largely my fault.

As their father, it is my job to see that their interests are broad and encompassing. I need to actively look for new and different hobbies to introduce to my children. And when they do show an interest in something, I need to encourage them to pursue it further. I want to teach them to dream big dreams and then work toward accomplishing those dreams.

At best, I'll be helping my children find their life calling, and at worst, I'll have spent a little more time with my kids. Either way, nobody loses.

A MESSAGE FOR KID-FRIENDLY MOMS

Debbie, my sister-in-law, didn't know a softball from a turnip before she married Mike. She had never wanted to play eighteen holes of golf, and camping was definitely not on her list of ways to spend a fun weekend. But today she plays centerfield on a church softball team, has her own set of golf clubs and knows how to rough it in the great outdoors.

"I just couldn't bear the thought of him having fun when I wasn't around," she joked to me once. But actually she understood a basic principle for building healthy relationships. She knew how important sports were to her husband and wanted to share that part of his life with him.

Nothing will ruin a hobby more effectively than the feeling that your spouse resents it. Resentment will drive a wedge between a couple.

If you're looking for a great way to enhance your relationship with your husband, as well as create meaningful family times together, take an interest in some of his hobbies. Learn why he enjoys them so much. You may even find yourself enjoying golf more than he does! And hopefully he will discover that he enjoys some of your hobbies as well.

— 8 —
Sex Education Teacher

*O*UR CHILDREN ARE GOING TO FIND OUT ABOUT SEX FROM
*some source. Better that it be from us than from their
friends, their teachers or the bathroom walls in their
schools. If we want the information they receive to be accurate and
moral, then we should see that it comes from home.*

What subject could be more interesting than sex?

A friend once joked about buying a book on sex to help spice up his marriage. "Did it help?" someone asked.

"No, not really. But I can't wait to get home every night to read the book!"

Sex is unique. What other human activity can be so beautiful and bonding under the right circumstances, and yet so devastating and divisive under the wrong ones? What other topic can be so divine in the right hands, yet so vile and ugly in the wrong hands?

Sex can be the most wonderful, intimate act of love that two people can possibly share. It can be the most relationship-enhancing practice on earth. It can also be the most repulsive, exploitive conduct on earth.

At the wrong time and place, with the wrong motives and with the wrong people, it can be nothing short of devastating.

What kind of sex is wrong sex? If you believe in Scripture as your authority, there is little room for debate. It is any kind of sex outside of marriage.

Marriage should be honored by all, and the marriage bed kept pure, for God will judge the adulterer and all the sexually immoral. (Hebrews 13:4)

Flee from sexual immorality. All other sins a man commits are outside his body, but he who sins sexually sins against his own body. Do you not know that your body is a temple of the Holy Spirit, who is in you, whom you have received from God? You are not your own; you were bought at a price. Therefore honor God with your body. (1 Corinthians 6:18-20)

The Pain of Lost Innocence

I'm proud of many things I've done in my life. Though I'm not the most disciplined or accomplished person, I've had some successes. But of all the things I can boast of, only one makes me truly proud and thankful. I went into our marriage pure—a virgin. I remained true to my beliefs and abstained from sex before marriage.

That makes me happy. And it makes me even happier to say that Ruthie showed the same conviction. She, too, honored the marriage bed.

It's wonderful to be able to say that. Though we married relatively late in life, we both came into the relationship undefiled. Pure. Amateurs. Neither of us had been—or have been—with other partners. When we lie together at night, no skeleton from the past, no guilt or shame or remorse accompanies us. No comparisons. Only us.

Of course, I'm painfully aware that many solid, Christian married couples cannot say that. I have no intent of laying a guilt trip on those couples. Many have done an admirable job of working through their past and going on to have a wonderful, beautiful marriage. I'm not pointing fingers. But I am trying to make an important point: God's will for couples to remain celibate until marriage is not an arbitrary command made by a stick-in-the-mud Creator. It is a directive with our happiness and self-image in mind. The charge is for our benefit, not his.

People aren't equipped to handle the emotional baggage that premarital sex brings into a marriage. We inevitably have a harder time forgiving ourselves than God has forgiving us. And few sins weigh heavier on a Christian than the guilt of sexual immorality.

It is of overwhelming importance to me that my children understand the emotional consequences of sex outside of marriage. I want them to know how damaging a single sexual encounter can be to their self-esteem, to their relationship with God and to their future earthly relationships. I want them to understand clearly how good they will feel about themselves and their future marriage if they can remain true and pure and faithful.

Nothing makes me sadder than stories such as the one I heard recently from a renowned family counselor. A sixteen-year-old girl was sent to him for counseling, and while there described her first sexual encounter at the age of thirteen. "I was so tired of hearing about sex from my friends and wanted to know what it was like for myself," she began. "So at a party I went up to the cutest guy I could find and asked him if he wanted to do it." The two of them went into a bedroom, and in a matter of moments this young, innocent girl had lost her virginity. "It wasn't what I expected," she told the counselor. "But at least I knew what it was like and was able to talk about it with my friends."

She then went on to describe a string of sexual encounters over the next few years. Her lifestyle became more and more promiscuous as she continued to experiment with sex. And with each encounter her self-image—as well as her reputation—deteriorated further. She ended her meeting with the counselor by summarizing her feelings. "I know I'm still young, but I feel really old."

What painful emotional baggage that poor girl carries. And she will struggle with it for the rest of her life.

Helping Children Remain Pure

It would break my heart to see my children take even a step toward that kind of fruitless path. As their father I plan to do everything within my power to protect them from that kind of pain—to help them remain pure and innocent sexually.

But how does a father do that? What can he do to impress on his children the importance of remaining pure? And how does he equip them to remain true to their conviction once they are persuaded to stay celibate?

1. *Be available, knowledgeable and honest.* The first and most obvious thing I can do as a father is to prepare myself for what will inevitably come. Even at a young age David has surprised us with questions about babies and bodies, boys and girls and the differences between the two. More than a few times Ruthie and I have had to tackle straightforward inquiries into the subject. And we expect Kandilyn to come to us with the same questions over the next few years. We're committed always to be prepared and to be honest.

I won't get into the specifics of what to say when, how much detail is too much and at which ages those details should become more detailed. There are books that can address those matters much better than I. I'll say only that we need to prepare ourselves for the questions to come and then tackle them head-on when they do.

We need to be available when those questions arise. We need to be honest in our responses. And we need to be comfortable and knowledgeable enough to answer them frankly and openly.

Our children are going to find out about sex from some source. Better that it be from us than from their friends, their teachers or the bathroom walls in their schools. If we want the information they receive to be accurate and moral, then we should see that it comes from home.

2. *Don't give Satan the upper hand.* I've been told that I can't raise my children in a bubble. To be honest, if I thought I could I would probably try. But we really can't shield our kids from every harmful influence that the world and Satan will impose on them.

Still, I see no reason to let my own wants and desires add even more temptation to their lives than they will already face. There is much I can do as a father to limit those influences, and I should be willing to do that whenever possible.

To be more specific, there are many worldly influences that Ruthie and I simply refuse to let into our household. We've made a conscious decision to do without them. We used to enjoy reading magazines such as *People* or *Us* to catch up on the latest Hollywood gossip. But some time ago we

Do you want your children learning about sex from their public school teachers? Read this account recorded by James Dobson before you decide.

"*Recently a student and his parent who visited our Focus on the Family headquarters offered to report the curriculum used in a psychology class at a high school in Newport Beach, California.*

"*The teacher allegedly exposed his class of co-ed sophomores to virtually every known perversion. . . . He covered subjects in such detail that I would not describe them in this book.*

"*Subsequently there was the usual visit from homosexual activists, presenting—and promoting—their lifestyles to wide-eyed sophomores. This kind of information has a dramatic effect on the minds of impressionable fifteen-year-old male and female students. I don't care how liberated we have become. That is unconscionable!*"

—*James Dobson and Gary Bauer,* **Children at Risk** *(Dallas: Word, 1990), pp. 46-47.*

realized just how unhealthy many of the views and agendas of those magazines were. Not an issue went by that didn't report on another trendy young couple having a "love child" or another marriage ending "amicably." Revolving-door relationships seemed somehow fashionable and expected.

Not only did we tire of supporting that type of reporting, but we also saw no reason to expose our children to those kinds of messages. Especially when they run counter to everything we teach and believe.

So we decided to stop buying them. Completely. Instead, we fill our magazine rack with good Christian periodicals.

We've also made some tough decisions regarding television. More than any other medium, TV has well overstepped the bounds of sexual decency. Even hardened producers will admit that programming has often gone too far. Couple that with the fact that TV is the most influential medium in our culture, and you have quite a problem on your hands.

An MTV executive was recently asked in an interview what effect the network's programming had on the youth of today. "We don't have an effect on youth," he answered. "We *own* the youth."

MTV may very well have an enormous influence on our culture, but it does not, will not and will never *own* the youth of the Martin household. Television may be a staple in America, but it will forever remain an occasional treat in our home. Today, in fact, our TV is sitting in the garage collecting dust. We may drag it indoors for the occasional football game, and may even rent a movie to watch as a family, but afterward it will go right back where it belongs—out of sight and out of mind.

Many worldly influences will have only as much impact on our kids as we choose to allow. And in the effort to keep our kids pure, it seems only wise to greatly limit the temptations they will face.

3. *Model a healthy relationship in the home.* Someone once said that the best way to tell if a stick is crooked is to hold it up next to a straight one.

In a world filled with unhealthy relationships and unhappy marriages, it's no wonder so many are confused about sex and romance. If we want our children to understand and appreciate intimacy in marriage, we need to give them a clear model of a right relationship—a straight stick to hold up next to all of the crooked ones.

I'll never forget the many times I saw Dad embrace Mom from behind while she was cooking or cleaning or doing the dishes. She would smile and pretend to brush him off, then turn to give him a kiss.

They'd whisper to each other and then go about their business. There was no doubt that they were crazy about each other—that they were attracted physically as well as emotionally. And the message they were sending was one of comfort and security and respect in a relationship.

Educating children about sex is so much more than imparting a few facts about birds and bees and boys and girls. It is teaching children how to be caring and romantic and loving. How we view our spouses and how we treat them in the home will have an enormous impact on our children's view of themselves and their sexuality. And it will be the basis by which they choose their future partners.

If our daughters see us treating their mothers with respect and dignity, that is how they will expect to be treated. If our sons see us loving and caring for their mothers, they will grow to be loving, caring husbands.

4. *Instill in them a desire to remain chaste.* Ultimately, the decision to either remain chaste or engage in sexual activity rests with our children. Though many of us would like to make that choice for them, we know we can't. As in many other areas of their lives, we need to give them the tools to make the right decisions and then pray that they will have the strength and courage and heart to do the right thing when the time comes. We must raise them to be trustworthy and then step back and trust them.

During my high-school years I had several opportunities to experiment with sex. Though kids were much less active sexually during those days than they seem to be today, a boy could still find what he wanted if he wanted it. One time, in fact, I was propositioned in no uncertain terms. She had the time, the place and the desire; all I needed to do was agree. Thankfully, I didn't. I chose not to. And I didn't even feel the need to explain myself.

I could point to many factors in my life that led to that decision. I felt good enough about myself—both as a person and as a child of God—that I didn't need to "prove myself" to others. It was very clear to me, even at a young age, that sex before marriage, and outside of marriage, was simply wrong. I wasn't overwhelmed with the fear of disease or the fear of becoming a father. Those kinds of things could be prevented. I simply knew it was wrong. It was a sin before God. Plain and simple.

But perhaps the strongest influence on my decision to abstain was a deep sense of purpose and direction. I had many goals and desires for my future, and a one-night-stand simply didn't fit into those plans. I refused to be deterred. I didn't want to jeopardize my future.

We can go a long way toward helping our children remain pure by instilling in them a healthy self-esteem and a strong sense of purpose—to help them develop goals solid enough to keep them focused.

5. *Help them develop "hedges" against sexual temptation.* Jerry Jenkins has written an insightful book entitled *Hedges: Loving Your Marriage Enough to Protect It.* The premise is simple: The surest way to remain faithful to our marriage partner is to create hedges in our lives to shield us from the temptation of straying. In the book he outlines some "hedges" he has set up for himself, and he encourages others to follow suit.

His idea is ingenious. And with a little modification it can be used as an invaluable tool for helping our children overcome the temptations to sin sexually. When our children reach an appropriate age, we should help them set up some hedges against sexual temptation, and then encourage them to stick by their hedges unconditionally. One hedge might be to limit the amount of time they will let themselves be alone with a date, or to determine how long they should need to know someone before deciding to date that person. They would definitely need to set limits on what kind of parties and outings they will allow themselves to attend.

Helping children set up hedges is good because it puts the emphasis on *them*, not their parents. We should make it clear that these are *their* hedges to establish, not just arbitrary rules set by their parents. It lays the responsibility for purity on their shoulders, where it belongs.

James Dobson once told of a similar idea. When his children reached a certain age, he took them alone to a quiet, pre-scheduled place. Once there, he reminded them of his desire for them to remain pure before marriage and explained the reasons once again. He also explained the concept of vows and what it means to make a vow to God. He then encouraged them to bow with him, right then and there, and vow before God that they would remain true to their future marriage partner—that they would abstain from sex regardless of the temptations and pressures they might face.

> **Ten Common Excuses Fathers Make for Not Talking to Their Kids About Sex**
> *1. The kids are too young; I need to wait a few years.*
> *2. Women are better at those kinds of things.*
> *3. I'm too embarrassed.*
> *4. I don't want to embarrass my kids.*
> *5. They won't understand.*
> *6. I didn't know anything when I was their age, and it worked for me.*
> *7. They might ask me a question I can't answer.*
> *8. They haven't asked me yet.*
> *9. They might say something in front of my mother.*
> *10. They'll find out when they get married anyway.*

Afterward, he presented them with a key on a chain—something they could wear as a reminder of their vow and a symbol of the covenant they had made before God.

What a wonderful idea. Since hearing about it, Ruthie and I have decided to do the same with our children when they are older.

A Child with a Heart for God

Sex before marriage is an exciting prospect. There's not a boy or girl who hasn't wondered what it would be like "just this once." The temptation and pressure to experiment can often be immense—even more so today than in days gone by.

I hope to be sensitive to my kids as they go through those times. When they feel tempted to sway, I hope they will come to me. When they want advice, I hope they look for it at home. When they want acceptance and love, I hope they find an abundance of it right in their own living room.

But more than that, I hope that their relationship with God is stronger than their urge to sin. And I hope that they feel good enough about themselves to remain true to their convictions—to remain pure and undefiled until marriage.

What more could a father ask?

A MESSAGE FOR KID-FRIENDLY MOMS

Let's face it—dads are good at many things, but they are seldom good at talking with their kids about sex. Most fathers would rather stick needles in their eyes than sit down and answer direct questions about reproduction from an inquisitive six-year-old. In our heart of hearts, we know it's something we need to do, but that seldom makes it any easier.

Mothers can do a world of good by taking it upon themselves to "fill in the gaps" for their children. If Dad is having a hard time explaining the art of "pollination," don't wait too long before stepping in and helping out.

Also, modeling romance is a two-way street. It's important for your children to see a fair amount of parental affection around the house. But not all guys are comfortable with those kinds of public displays. And not all husbands remember its importance—both to you and to your kids.

Don't be afraid to sit down and remind Dad of your needs and your children's budding attitudes about sex and romance. And don't be afraid to take the initiative yourself and chase Dad around the house sometime!

— 9 —
Courtship
Counselor

*I*F WE WANT OUR KIDS TO FEEL GOOD ABOUT THEMSELVES AND TO
   have a happy, productive and successful life, it is crucial that
   we teach them how to choose the right marriage partner—and
that we give them the tools they need to make that decision.

Pretend that it's ten, fifteen or twenty years from now, and you are
sitting in the front row of a church, watching your daughter's wedding
ceremony. You've just marched her down the aisle, said your line to
the minister and placed her hand in the hand of her husband-to-be.
Your wife, who is sitting next to you, has long since drenched your
handkerchief with tears, and you're fighting back a few of your own.

Then comes the time for your daughter's vows. You listen intently
as she promises to love, honor and stand by her new husband through
sickness, health, poverty, wealth, bad times and good times, until death
does them part. Rings are exchanged. More tears fall. The consum-
mating kiss sends murmurs of approval through the crowd. And
finally, the minister pronounces them husband and wife, and they walk
arm in arm down the long aisle to the foyer in the back.

During the reception, you want desperately to take your daughter aside for a few moments and tell her all of the things you wished you had told her earlier. But there is no time. Between the photographer, the guests, the cutting of the cake and the tossing of the bouquet, she has little time to even notice you are there.

Is she really ready for this? you ask yourself. Only yesterday, it seems, she was sitting on your lap listening to bedtime stories, and today she is all grown-up and getting married.

Then, to one side, you notice the groom. He seems so young. His smile is awkward in front of the cameras, and his long, thin arms hang a few inches too long for the sleeve of his jacket. *He's just a boy,* you think to yourself. *Is he going to be able to support my little girl?*

You remember how you've grown to like the boy over the last few months. The first impression wasn't the best, but in time he seemed likable enough. You gave the relationship six months at the most, the pattern of her previous relationships. Now it is two years later, and you realize how wrong you were.

After the reception, you find yourself standing outside of the church while the two of them make the traditional mad dash to the car. With rice flying and crowds cheering, you make your way to the car to say one last goodby to your little girl.

"I'll call you tomorrow, Daddy," she says.

"Don't forget," you answer. "I'll be waiting." The door closes, the car starts and inches its way into the street, and you stand waving as the two of them drive off.

That's when it hits you the hardest.

Who is this boy driving away with my daughter? you ask yourself. *What do I know about him? How will he treat her? What kind of husband and father will he be?*

You've known for years that this day would eventually come, but now that it's here you want it to go away. All you've ever wanted is to make her happy forever, and now that fate is no longer in your hands. It's in the hands of a young, scrawny boy you hardly know and she's convinced she's in love with.

Does fatherhood get any more frightening than this?

A Relationship for Life

If you have a daughter, you've probably already envisioned this scene. There's hardly a father among us who doesn't worry about what kind of people his children will eventually grow to marry. We wonder what they will be like, what kind of family and background they will come from and, most important, how they will treat their mate—our child.

We also wonder what kind of marriage partners our kids themselves will be. We hope they grow to be the kind of husbands, wives, mothers and fathers that we try to be.

Every father has to face the task of teaching his kids how to pick the right kind of mate. Of all the things we hope to pass on to our kids, this one belongs at the top of the list—second only to their relationship with God. We know it, and we want desperately to see that they know it. Their marriage will forever be the second most important relationship in their lives. And if they blow it—if they pick the wrong mate—it will affect every other relationship they have, including their most important one.

Choosing the Right Mate

I know a man from my college days who picked the wrong mate (a subjective opinion, but one that few who know him would argue

> "Marriage is more than finding the right person. It is being the right person."
>
> —Anonymous

with) and is now living with the consequences.

Warren seemed destined to be a great leader in the church. At a young age he showed an interest in preaching and set out to follow that calling. Even in college he had a fiery way with words in the pulpit and an uncanny grasp of theology.

But then he met and married Patricia. Patricia liked Warren, but she didn't like preachers. They didn't bring in the kind of income she wanted, so she quickly determined that preaching wasn't Warren's calling to begin with and tried to change his mind.

Soon after their marriage, Warren quit preaching and went into business. He still taught adult classes at church, until Patricia convinced him that he didn't have time for such things. So he gave that up as well. Today, Warren resigns himself to putting in a good attendance record at church and working on his business ventures. He's still a good man, but those who know him well—and many who don't—say he's not happy.

I can't help but wonder how things might have been had he ignored his wife's groanings and pursued his career in ministry instead. Or if he had picked another wife—someone who would support his dreams and talents rather than subvert them.

In contrast, I once heard a story about a New York City mayor of long ago. He was walking with his wife beside a store window when a man cleaning the glass called out to the mayor's wife. The two of them had dated years earlier and hadn't seen each other for quite some time. After a short visit, the mayor and his wife said their goodbys. As they walked away, he turned to her and said, "Isn't it funny—if you had married him, today you'd be the wife of a window cleaner."

She smiled and without hesitation answered, "No, if I had married him, today he'd be the mayor of New York."

I like that story because it highlights the importance of choosing the right mate. And it puts teeth into the old adage "Beside every successful man is a good woman."

If we want our kids to feel good about themselves and to have a happy, productive and successful life, it is crucial that we teach them how to choose the right marriage partner—and that we give them the tools they need to make that decision.

Steering Kids Toward the Right People

As a teenager, I'm sure I gave my parents many worries. Like most teens, I struggled with the pains and uncertainties of growing up, and they struggled right along with me. But nowhere did they worry more about me than in the area of relationships. They worried about what kinds of kids I was running around with—who my friends were, who my friends' friends were and mostly what kind of girls I was dating.

For the most part my judgment was sound enough. Most of the girls I dated were decent girls with proper reputations. But there was one exception.

Katie was a bright, pretty girl who caught my eye in the tenth grade. She was new in town, new in school, and soon began attending our church, so I made my move and within a few weeks we were dating. What I didn't know was that Katie's reputation had followed her. Our town was small, and the town she moved from was even smaller. The news traveled fast.

What I also didn't know was that she was trying hard to shake that reputation—without necessarily reforming her ways. So the only side of Katie I saw was the sweet, innocent side. Our relationship was as harmless as I was (pretty harmless!). But people were starting to wonder.

Meanwhile, my parents had made a point of finding out everything they could about the girls I spent time with. It didn't take them long to decide that Katie

Here are some ideas for teaching your children about healthy dating relationships.

■ *Make a date with your teenage daughter. And do it right. Call her from work one day and set the time and date. Let her pick the restaurant and the movie. And don't use the time to talk to her about parent-child kinds of things. Let this be her night, not your opportunity to lecture. (Moms, you can do the same with your teenage sons.)*

■ *When your kids get old enough to start "going steady," invite them and their girlfriend/boyfriend to double-date with you and your wife. Then be on your best behavior. Let them see firsthand what a truly healthy (and Christian) romantic relationship is like.*

■ *Most all of our kids have seen their parents argue. But too often when we do, we make up in private, when the kids are not around. If we're going to argue in front of the kids, we should also let them see us apologize and make up. It's an uncomfortable thought, but it can also be a valuable lesson in right relationships.*

was dangerous. The stage seemed set for a showdown between my parents and me. If I were to find myself in their shoes now, I might be inclined to shoot first and ask questions later.

But they didn't. They seemed to like Katie as much as I did. They had her over for dinner at every opportunity and spoke nothing but good about her around me. As far as I knew, it was business as usual.

All the while, my parents watched, worried and prayed.

Three or four weeks into our relationship, I began feeling uncomfortable around Katie. I sensed that she was hiding something from me—something serious. And I sensed that she was a bit more experienced in life than the other girls I had dated. I didn't dare talk to Katie about it, but I felt I should talk to someone. Given my parents' acceptance and trust in me in the past, I decided to go to them.

That day, after talking with my parents about my concerns, I decided to break off the relationship—still not knowing what they knew about her. All I knew was, I felt uncomfortable around her, and I chose to bow out. The decision was mine.

I'm still amazed when I think of how well my parents handled the situation. In spite of their worries, and in spite of their knowledge of Katie's past, they remained true to their trust in me. When they saw me heading for trouble, they kept a close watch and stayed on their knees, but they didn't reach out to stop me. They instead saw that I had the vision to see the trouble coming and the wherewithal to stop myself when it did.

Pick Your Friends—Don't Let Your Friends Pick You

And where did the vision and the wherewithal come from? Something my parents had said to me in a hundred different ways over the years, something they reiterated in our conversation that day.

"If you don't feel good about her, you don't have to date her," they told me. "It's just that simple. You're much too good a person to settle for less than you want in a girl."

When I told them of my concerns about Katie, they didn't try to step in and make my mind up for me. They didn't set down rules or ultimatums regarding my relationships. They simply relayed their trust in my instincts and my spiritual maturity and left me to make the decision for myself. And then they prayed that I would make the right choice.

This lesson stuck with me more than any other when it came to relationships, and has proved to be the most beneficial. My parents taught me to pick my friends, not to let my friends pick me. Whether the relationship was a casual acquaintance, a good friendship, a weekend date or a potential marriage partner, the principle remained always in my mind. When I didn't enjoy being around someone, when we didn't click, when our values and beliefs differed, I was cordial and polite, but I didn't get involved.

"It's just that simple. You're much too good a person to settle for less than you want . . ."

That's a lesson I want my kids to learn. They should pick their friends, not let their friends pick them.

The Right Kind of Marriage

The reasoning follows that if we teach our kids to pick their friends, it is just as important that they learn to pick the right kinds of friends. Most important of all, we need to show them how to pick the right kind of mate.

During my teenage years I understood that the right marriage partner meant first and foremost a Christian woman, someone whose values and trust in God superseded everything else in her life. And that is the kind of woman I married.

But today, more and more kids from Christian homes are marrying non-Christians. It no longer "goes without saying" that marriage partners should share the same faith, so I feel compelled to say it. If we want our kids to marry well, we must instill in them a deep need to find a partner of shared faith—someone who is "equally yoked" with them spiritually. Someone who believes in the same God of creation that they believe in, and who has given his or her life over to him. Someone with whom they can pray and study and talk about scriptural truths. If they settle for anything less, they will feel the consequences for the rest of their lives, no matter how much they feel love can conquer and overcome.

Our children won't know what pain is until they have to dress their children by themselves on Sunday morning and sit with them alone at church while their mate sleeps in till noon; until they have to work alone at the task of saving their children's souls; until they feel forced into a divorce by a spouse who has run off with someone else; or until they have to bury an unbelieving spouse, aware of his or her eternal fate.

I wouldn't wish that kind of pain on anyone, especially my children.

A Father's Example

When it comes time for my children to start looking for a marriage partner, I hope they use criteria that go far beyond appearance and status. I want them to search for someone who is kind and caring, stable emotionally and spiritually, honest and sincere, and primarily concerned about the needs of others. I want them to find partners who feel good about themselves and their choices—and who know how to treat others with respect and love too. More than that, I want my children to *be* that kind of person. I want them to be a joy to live with.

But if I hope to see that wish-list fulfilled, I need to start setting the stage now, here in my own life and family. If I want my son to learn how to treat women with respect and dignity, and if I want my daughter to look for that kind of man, I had better treat their mother that way. If I want my children to have high self-esteem, I need to start by seeing that I am the kind of father who fosters self-respect in his family. If Ruthie and I love and respect each other, and love and respect ourselves, then our children will likely feel the same. And they will look for that quality in a marriage partner.

The relationship that Ruthie and I share will be the model for our children's relationships. How we treat each other is how they will likely treat their own mates. Our example, whether good or bad, will have an impact on every future relationship they have.

Some time ago I realized I wasn't setting the right kind of example in this area. Ruthie, who is more patient with me than she should be, came down to my office one day and closed the door. I could tell she had something she wanted to talk about. In her gentle way, she explained to me that David was watching me much more closely than I realized, and he was starting to talk to her, and treat her, in many of the same ways that I was.

So what's the problem? I thought (which shows how dense I can be sometimes).

She went on to explain that though I probably didn't mean any harm, in little ways I was treating her with disrespect and now David was starting to do the same. Often, when we finished

How are you at modeling a healthy marriage relationship for your kids? Are you treating your wife with the respect she deserves? If so, why are so many wives burdened with a poor self-image?

In a survey conducted at a recent men's retreat, 95 percent of the men believed their wives to have low self-esteem. Here are some of their reasons:

■ *60 percent noticed their wives putting themselves down on a regular basis.*

■ *45 percent said their wives didn't initiate close friendships.*

■ *40 percent believed their wives to be perfectionists when it came to the kids.*

■ *35 percent seldom if ever initiated romance for fear of rejection.*

■ *25 percent were not comfortable accepting compliments.*

—*Adapted from Greg Johnson and Mike Yorkey,* Daddy's Home *(Wheaton, Ill: Tyndale House, 1992), p. 70.*

Most of us could do much better when it comes to helping our wives feel good about themselves. If we want our children to see firsthand what a healthy husband-wife relationship looks life, we need to take a good look at how we are acting and reacting toward our mates.

eating lunch or dinner I would get up without saying a word, take my glass down to the office and resume working. "I know it sounds like a little thing," she explained, "but it would be nice if you helped clear the table and perhaps thanked me for the dinner."

I felt smaller by the minute.

"It's not that I need to hear you say it, but our kids do. They need to know that you appreciate what I do around the house."

The fact is, she needs to hear it as much as they do. It was wrong of me to assume otherwise.

That very afternoon while walking through the hallway to the kitchen I heard Ruthie scolding David for something he had done wrong. "What's going on?" I asked.

"Oh, Mom's just having a bad day," David answered. "She'll get over it."

I knew right then that I needed to work on a lot more than clearing the table and saying thanks for the dinner.

Even in the smallest areas of our lives, our kids are watching and imitating us. If Ruthie and I argue and bicker, our kids will become argumentive and bickering people. If Ruthie and I don't respect and love each other openly, our kids will be disrespectful and unloving in their relationships.

When it comes to guiding my children in their coming courtship views and practices, there is one all-encompassing, all-important thing I need to do: love and cherish their mother.

The rest should fall into place rather naturally.

A MESSAGE FOR KID-FRIENDLY MOMS

It really is true that "beside every great man is a good woman." As trite and old-fashioned as that saying sounds, it has proven to be as accurate and valid as anything I've heard. We guys don't always admit it, but we really are better off with you than without you.

I sincerely doubt that I would have ever taken the time and initiative to write my first book had Ruthie not been there to encourage me and cheer me on throughout the process. Every step of the way she has been there to keep me going. Her belief in me is truly an inspiration.

Not only is that an encouragement to me, but it's an invaluable example for our children. I want my daughter to learn firsthand the value of a relationship built on mutual respect and admiration—to see how beautiful a marriage can be when two people work to bring out the best in each other. And I want my son to know how wonderful it can be to have a wife who believes in him and encourages him to be the best he can be.

If they see that kind of relationship in their parents' marriage, they will likely create that kind of relationship in their own.

Every man needs a good woman. Because good women always seem to bring out the best in a man.

—10—
Model of Masculinity

*T*HE MOST SOBERING, GUT-WRENCHING, SWEAT-PRODUCING *concept on earth is that we fathers are seen by our children as the earthly counterparts of God. How can we possibly measure up?*

Being the only male role model in the home is no small matter.

How my son views himself and his role in society, in the home, in the church and in his marriage directly relates to what he sees in me. How my daughter relates to every future man in her life depends greatly on how she views her relationship with me. Even more significant, how my children eventually relate to God—how they view his anger, his love, his compassion, his guidance—depends largely on what they see in their father.

Now that's a sobering thought. It should scare the wits out of any father who truly understands the implications. I don't remember reading that in the job description when my kids were born. It's more responsibility than most of us signed on for, isn't it?

Still, it is a fact—and a mandate—we must learn to live with. More than that, one that we must learn to live up to!

A few days ago I listened to a young man talking about the struggles he was having in his marriage. He had been a husband less than two years and a father for just over five months. But knowing how to act and who he should be in those roles puzzled him.

"My father was a preacher, and everyone talked about how spiritual he was," he explained. "And maybe he was a spiritual person. But he wasn't a very good father. He was never there for us when we needed him. The church always came first. He gave all of his time and energy to those people and had little left for us."

> "A child is not likely to find a father in God unless he finds something of God in his father."
>
> —Austin L. Sorensen

Through tears the young man described how hard it was to be a good father to his young boy. "I just hope I can be there for him," he said. "But when the time comes, I'm afraid I won't know how."

How few of us truly understand the important role our lives and values play in the future of our children. We seldom realize the magnitude of our influence. If we hope to raise godly, healthy Christian men and women, we must take a long, hard look at our own lives. And we must ask ourselves some deep questions about who we are as men, as fathers, as husbands and as Christians.

Becoming a Godly Man

What is a man's role in his marriage, family, church and career? What does it mean to be truly masculine? How do we go about modeling godly principles and practices to our children? What does it mean to be a godly man?

Bill McCartney, head coach of the University of Colorado Buffaloes, has been one of the most outspoken Christians in the country about the role of men in society. In his book *What Makes a Man?* he outlines what he calls the "three non-negotiables of manhood: *integrity, commitment and action.*"

In his words, a godly man is "a guy who, when he says something, can be trusted. When he gives his word, you can take it to the bank. His word is good."[1] I like that definition, because it expresses what I believe would be God's definition of a truly masculine man.

A Man of Integrity

A line in a movie I saw long ago has stayed with me. The film was *And Justice for All,* starring Al Pacino as an attorney. In one scene he was talking with his nearly senile grandfather. His grandfather said, "Tell me, son, are you an honest lawyer?"

Pacino's character stared at the ground for a second, then replied, "Well, grandfather, I've found that being honest doesn't have much to do with being a lawyer."

The grandfather looked him squarely in the eyes and said, "If you're not honest, you're not anything."

What a powerful impact we could have on the world and our families if every one of us held to that credo. What a statement we'd be making about ourselves and our faith.

Sadly, that's not always the case. Too many of us find it easier and more profitable (at least in the short term) to be a little dishonest.

> **Rate yourself from 1 to 10 for each question below, which are based on Bill McCartney's criteria for a godly man. A perfect score is 60.**
>
> *A Godly Man Is a Man of . . .*
> *Integrity:*
> *1. My kids know me as an honest man. _____*
> *2. I tell the truth to my family, even when it hurts. _____*
> *Commitment:*
> *3. I don't break promises to my wife and kids. _____*
> *4. I would never leave my wife, no matter how bad things get in our marriage. _____*
> *Action:*
> *5. I take the lead in the spiritual development of my family. _____*
> *6. When my family needs me, I am there, regardless of what other demands are made on my time. _____*
> *If you scored a perfect 60, congratulations. You can stop reading now and skip to the next chapter!*

Whenever I think of integrity—or the lack of it—I think of a story I heard about a father and his son. The family car had been in a slight fender-bender, and the dad took his son with him to gather three estimates for the insurance company. The first estimator was surveying the damage when he stopped and turned to the father. "So, what kind of deductible are you looking at?" he asked.

"It's five hundred out of my pocket," the father answered. "That is, unless you can help me out with that a little."

"I think we can work something out," the man answered with a wry grin.

The estimator finished the appraisal, then handed a copy to the father. "Let me give you the names of a couple of friends of mine. Their shops are just a few blocks from here. You show them that estimate and tell them I sent you and they'll fix you up."

Dad smiled knowingly. "I'll do that. Thanks for the help."

As they were driving off, the boy asked, "Dad, what does *deductible* mean? And what did that guy mean when he said these other men would 'fix you up'?"

Try explaining that one, Dad! Your boy is watching, and he really wants to know. A godly man, if he is anything at all, is honest—a man of integrity.

A Man of Commitment

I used to do business with a man who had a favorite phrase. "You've got to walk like you talk," he'd say adamantly. "If you say you're going to do something, you do it. Otherwise, you'll never last in business."

That's an important concept, but not always easy or convenient to carry out—especially in our families. Trying to balance our time between work, home, church and friends is demanding for any man. It calls for many commitments. Most of those commitments we keep—some for fear of losing our job, others for fear of losing our standing in the church, and still others for fear of losing friends. But how easily we forget to keep the commitments we make to our family. Not big ones, but little, everyday, seemingly insignificant ones.

Earlier this afternoon my son asked if I would play his marble game with him. "Sure I will," I told him. "But we have a lot of other things to do first."

And we did. My in-laws are coming to visit next week, and I promised my wife that I would help get the house ready for them. Some closets and drawers needed cleaning out, furniture needed rearranging, pictures needed hanging—the normal getting-ready-for-company kinds of things.

The whole family pitched in, and after a few hours we had things pretty much under control—at about David's bedtime. I was tired, and for a few minutes I considered putting him to bed and playing the game with him tomorrow. It was a tempting thought, and he would forgive me.

But that would have been wrong. In my heart I knew it. I had made a commitment, and now it was time to follow through, no matter how tired I was, how late it was or how much writing I still needed to do. David may have missed his usual bedtime, but at least he went to bed knowing his dad kept his commitment.

A Man of Action

Nothing can do more damage to the emotional and physical health of a family than an apathetic, spiritually lazy father.

So many fathers today have relinquished the spiritual development of their families to their wives. "Women are more in tune to those kinds of things," they say. "I'll make a good living for us and teach the boys to play ball, but the wife's going to have to teach them about the Bible."

How I feel for the woman who has to live with a spiritually apathetic husband.

A godly man is a man of action, one who will take the reins and lead his family—emotionally, physically, financially and spiritually. He looks for ways to minister to his wife and kids, and when he sees a need, he fills it.

When he sees his kids wasting their time—and precious brain cells—watching mindless garbage on TV, he doesn't sit down and join them. He turns the set off, gathers his family in a circle and holds an impromptu devotional or discussion.

When he sees his wife getting nowhere trying to clean the kitchen with kids tugging at her shirt, he doesn't slip away to the den to read the paper. He mobilizes the troops. He pitches in to help and makes cleaning a family affair.

Being Sensitive to the Needs of Our Kids

Being a godly man also means learning to be sensitive to the feelings and needs of those around us—especially (though not exclusively) our children.

Darrell, a business associate, is a good father to his kids in many ways. Though he works too many hours, he does try to spend most of his free time with his wife and kids. He takes them to games, coaches Little League when he can, and makes it to most of their school functions. He's also a strict disciplinarian (too strict, perhaps), so his kids are exceptionally well-behaved in public.

Darrell could do better on many fronts—I'm close enough to him and his situation to know that. But the one area of fathering he needs to work on the hardest is his basic lack of sensitivity. Not a lack of love, mind you, because in that department his heart overflows. The problem is more how he displays—or doesn't display—that love.

One particular incident stands out in my mind. I happened to be at his house, going over some business issues. We were sitting at the kitchen table while his children were drawing pictures in the next room. Darrell was on the phone when Chad, his six-year-old, came running into the room with a picture he had drawn.

"Look, Daddy—look at the picture I drew," he said excitedly. Darrell quickly scolded him for interrupting his call and told him to wait until he was finished.

Chad waited patiently by his side; then as soon as Darrell hung up the phone, he again held his picture up. "Look what I drew for you, Daddy," he repeated.

Darrell took the picture and laid it face down on the table. "Chad, haven't we talked about what happens when you interrupt Daddy when he's on the phone?"

Chad nodded, eyes aimed at the floor.

"So, what do you think we need to do about it?"

"Punish me," Chad answered.

"That's right. I don't want to punish you, but I have to. You know, Daddy gets important phone calls at home, and I can't be interrupted . . ." Darrell continued to lecture Chad for the next few minutes. From time to time, Chad would glance up at the picture on the table, then look downward.

C'mon, Darrell, I thought to myself, *give the kid a break and look at the picture!*

A few minutes later, after he felt sure Chad had understood the seriousness of his transgression, he handed him back his picture and sent him back into the other room.

"I won't punish you this time, Chad. But don't forget what we talked about."

Chad walked away, limply carrying the picture in one hand to his side, as Darrell picked up the phone to make another call. Never once did he even glance at the picture that Chad made for him. I wish now that I had said something, but I didn't.

I'm sure Darrell thought he was doing the right thing. After all, kids need to learn not to interrupt. He's right about that. From what I've seen, too many parents have forgotten to teach such basic courtesies to their kids. But in the midst of his mission to raise polite children, he is forgetting to be sensitive to their needs and feelings. He's forgetting how tender and fragile children's egos can be, and how much they crave and need their father's approval.

A kid-friendly dad learns to be sensitive to the needs and struggles of his kids.

Being Sensitive to the Needs of Our Wives

I also hope I will learn to show more sensitivity to my wife. I say "will learn" because I haven't been very skilled at it over the years. I'm better than I was, but I'm certainly not where I need or want to be.

For instance, I remember a time early in our marriage where I showed a great deal of insensitivity toward Ruthie.

We had been invited to a party, and were both looking forward to it. The afternoon of the event, however, Ruthie came down with a fever. It was slight at first, and we thought we'd still be able to attend. But as the day progressed, her fever rose. By evening she was running a temperature of 102, feeling sick to her stomach and shivering. She said she had a bad case of the flu.

I wasn't convinced, however; I thought she was letting a slight bug get the best of her. My first reaction was that she should just pull herself together and go anyway. "It can't be that bad," I told her. "And as soon as we get home you can take some medicine and go to sleep for as long as you like." Surely, I thought, she was "man enough" to handle a little cold for one evening out.

Wrong answer.

I'd like to say that I've completely reformed since then, but I know better. I still have a lot to learn about showing sensitivity when she's sick or in need of sympathy.

Most of us need to do better when it comes to showing sensitivity to our wives.

Being Sensitive to the Needs of Others

Just as in every other area of our lives, our children are watching closely how we relate to others. If we hope to instill in them a caring, sensitive heart, we must first look deep into our own.

Whenever I think of sensitivity, my friend Wes comes to mind—a young husband and father in our church. I've heard many positive words about him over the years. People in our church family know that if they need a helping hand, a listening ear or an understanding word, they can always count on Wes.

Just a few weeks ago I was talking with his wife, Michele, and I commented on Wes's good heart and sensitive manner. "What is his secret?" I asked her.

"I wish I knew," she answered. "It amazes me how he always thinks of the needs of others before considering his own needs. And he doesn't do it out of a sense of guilt or duty like most of us—he simply loves to help others."

She went on to explain that this attitude characterized Wes's entire family. "His parents were able to instill in their kids an amazing mix of personal pride and humility at the same time. They are all very successful at their careers—and they all know it—yet they never seem to let that affect their attitudes about themselves and others. No matter how much they achieve in their lives, they are still very tuned in to the needs and feelings of others.

"Wes cares very deeply for people who are hurting and in need, and he usually acts on those feelings. And people know he is sincere. That's something you just can't fake."

Measuring Your S.Q.
Here's a test for measuring your "sensitivity quotient." Remember, no cheating!

1. When my wife has had a hard day with the kids, I . . .

a. Give her an extra pat on the back before heading for the driving range.

b. Tell her she should take a break just as soon as she finishes the dishes.

c. Send her to bed with a good book while I take the kids to McDonald's for supper.

2. When my teenage daughter comes home crying after breaking up with her boyfriend, I . . .

a. Tell her I've never liked the lazy slob anyway.

b. Pat her on the head and give her an extra dollar.

c. Sit and swing with her on the back porch as she tells me how much he meant to her. I might even tell her how I felt the first time I broke up with a girl.

3. When a church friend comes to me with a problem, I . . .

a. Give him a quarter for the phone and the name of a good counselor.

b. Tell him I'd have problems too if I had a wife like his.

c. Find a quiet place to sit and listen to his struggles.

NOTE: If you answered A or B to any of the above questions, you must now take a ruler and whack yourself on the head. Then keep reading and pay closer attention!

Wouldn't it be nice, I thought, if the world saw that kind of heart and attitude in the life of every Christian father? There's nothing more powerful and awesome than a man who has truly let the Spirit shape and mold him into a man of God. And there's no more effective model of masculinity.

Earthly Counterparts of God

A young father once asked rhetorically, "If God's character is to be understood in terms of my life, what does my child think of God?"[2]

The most sobering, gut-wrenching, sweat-producing concept on earth is that we fathers are seen by our children as the earthly counterparts of God. How can we possibly measure up? How can we even come close?

To think that my children are formulating their opinion of the Almighty based on the short-sighted, meager attempts of their earthly dad is intimidating, to say the least.

The good news is, through it all they seem to know that I'm *not* God—that I'm not perfect. And they're willing to overlook my shortcomings. I don't have to be everything that God is, I just have to be everything that I can be, with his help. I don't have to be perfect. I just have to love them the way that Christ loves me.

A MESSAGE FOR KID-FRIENDLY MOMS

My kids think I can do anything.

"Daddy, know what?" David asked the other day in the car.

"What, honey?"

"You're so strong I bet you could lift up that telephone pole!"

Ruthie smiled in my direction. "Well, I don't know if I'm quite that strong," I answered.

"Yes you could. I know you could. You can lift anything."

"You think so?" I inquired further.

"Yes you can. And I'll bet you could pick up that tree and move it too!"

"Well, maybe not *that* tree," I answered. Ruthie's smile widened. "Oh yes you can. You're so strong!"

My kids are also convinced that I can run faster, jump higher, work smarter and pray better than any man on earth. And it's Ruthie that has put them up to it. At every opportunity she builds me up in their eyes.

Every man wants to feel like a hero to his kids. We love hearing from our children about how strong and brave and wonderful we are. It makes us proud to be fathers. And also encourages us to want to live up to those qualities.

Mom, you can do wonders for your husband's image in the minds of your kids by looking for opportunities to build him up in their eyes. Talk to them about how hard Daddy works for the family and how much he loves God and how much he loves and cares for them.

Not only will you be helping your husband have a stronger influence in your children's lives, but you'll be inspiring him to want to be everything they think he is.

Now, if you'll excuse me, I've got a few trees in the yard I need to move . . .

—11—
Anchor in Times of Defiance

*D*URING TIMES OF DEFIANCE AND UNCERTAINTY—TIMES OF *high winds—I want to be the anchor that keeps my kids from drifting too far off center. I want to allow them the freedom to sway with the waves, but not to drift off. And like an anchor, I want to do it without fanfare, hidden far beneath the surface.*

I have a vivid memory from seventh grade. It was at one of our junior-high football games in a small stadium several blocks from our school.

At the time, I was tall and lanky with disproportionately large feet—size twelve, I think. I was wearing blue jeans and a matching jean jacket, a cowboy hat I borrowed from my dad (sorry, Dad, but I forgot to ask!), and a huge pair of pointed, steel-toed cowboy boots.

I remember walking the length of the stadium under the rafters, going nowhere in particular except maybe to see if I could spot someone I knew from school. To one side I noticed a rather pretty girl sitting on the bench watching me. I glanced at her, she smiled, and I smoothly nodded back, tipping my hat with my finger. Then quickly looking ahead again, I continued to walk, trying hard to look like a man who was no stranger to flirty glances. It wasn't easy, because I was.

The reason this scene stands out in my mind (besides the rare experience of being flirted with) is the fact that I felt so rough and manly. With my John Wayne-esque attire and my practiced strut, I truly felt I was the coolest, most rugged-looking kid in the place. Actually I was anything but rugged. But I felt that I looked the part, and figured that every boy there wished he were half the man I was at that moment. Looking back, it's rather embarrassing. I'm glad I don't have pictures of myself in that getup. The memories are laughable enough.

I remember another time several years later. I was standing in our back yard wearing a black imitation-leather jacket (we couldn't afford the real thing) and a glove with the fingers cut out. I was bouncing a racquetball off the side of the house—throwing it with my right hand and catching it with my left as it returned.

Why would I be wearing gloves and a jacket in the middle of summer in Texas? The day before, I had gone with some friends to see one of the Rocky movies—the second, I think. Rocky wore his famous leather jacket and gloves with the fingers cut out, and he bounced a racquetball everywhere he went. I can still hear the neighbors whispering, "Something strange about that Martin kid."

Still, I was convinced at the time that I was as cool as a northern breeze in Alaska. Ice cool. Until, that is, my brothers and sister came into the yard and put me in my place. They'd seen *Rocky* too, and I wasn't fooling anyone. They had a good laugh at my expense.

The Search for Identity
Most of us can easily relate to those kinds of memories. You no doubt have a few of your own. We all do, because we've all gone through times of searching for an identity. Some of us are still searching.

A large part of growing up is going through years of identity searches—of wondering what it would be like to do this or be that or wear our hair like so and so. One day a girl wears faded blue jeans and a torn sweater with her hair tousled and unkempt, and the next day she primps in front of the mirror for hours, worried about whether her nail polish matches her shoes. A boy works for weeks to grow his hair the perfect length for the newest style, then one day announces that he wants it cut short and slicked back with gel.

Fathers often think their kids are being fickle during these drastic changes, and in fact they are. But it's a natural part of growing up. The children are trying to find their identity. "Is this me?" they ask. "Is this my style, my personality?" And when they decide it isn't, they try something else.

The founders of the Minirth-Meier Clinic explain the internal ins and outs of what's going on:

The burgeoning child/adult has one leg firmly planted in a child-hood of little or no responsibility and the other leg in adulthood, craving the full responsibility accrued to an adult. . . .

Kids in early adolescence feel the urge to break away from the family, and yet they are afraid of leaving the nurturing nest. There's an enormous tug-of-war going on inside. . . .

So the kids test these limits by trying on different experimental lifestyles. They change their clothes and hair, and perhaps their mannerisms, to create a new look. It's all external, and they can thereby try out the lifestyle without actually investing much.

This experimentation is not conscious, in that the kids don't fully realize they're doing it. From Dad's viewpoint, they are shifting with the wind, blown this way and that by every idle breeze.[1]

The experts agree. Kids are fickle, and they have the right to be. Our job as fathers is to learn how to channel their fickleness—to see that they don't get blown too far by the wrong idle breezes.

For the most part, children tend to imitate who and what they admire the most at the time. A popular peer at school, the lead singer in a rock band, a movie star, a boss, a parent—whoever their heroes are, they want to be like them.

During my infamous strut through the bleachers in seventh grade, my family and friends knew that I had been watching too many John Wayne movies. My leather-jacket-and-racquetball episode was me wondering if my calling was to become a musclebound prize fighter.

Neither of those fantasies stuck with me for long, thank goodness. I'm far from a cowboy, and I bleed just staring at a boxing glove. But both roles played a small part in my childhood search for an identity. And as a father I want to remember those times. Because when my children go through the same struggles, I'll understand and give them room to experiment—within well-defined bounds, of course.

When All Is Said and Done

Having reflected on the pluses and minuses of this childhood identity searching, let me share a surprising observation. In spite of the many roles I experimented with in my life, the many different haircuts, fantasies, imitations and identity trials, in spite of the many times I took a defiant stand against my parents' rules and values, when I look at myself today I am still more like my father than anyone else. Though I never once remember actively trying to act and dress like Dad, never once holding him up as the person I wanted to emulate, he still has had the greatest impact on my identity. We are different in many ways, but my basic personality, my mannerisms, and my views on many issues look a lot like those of my father.

That can be a comforting observation, especially in an age where most actors, singers and celebrities are far from what I would consider good role models. I'm sure my father worried about me during my John Wayne- and Rocky-wannabe phases, but I tremble for the father who has to watch his kids dress and act like Prince or Ice-T or Madonna. It's a frightening thought, but one that each of us fathers has to worry about in the nineties.

Though there is no guarantee, the odds are in our favor that our children will eventually come around to the basic values and lifestyles of their parents. The concern we all have is, what irreparable harm will they have done to themselves by the time they "come around"? What consequences of their many lifestyle experiments will remain with them? A bad haircut will always grow out, clothes are as impermanent as things get, and even a tattoo can be removed, but children can never regain their virginity or erase a police record. Drug and alcohol abuse can lead to permanent harm. Consequences such as these will follow our children throughout their lives and affect their future, including their choices of college, career and marriage partner.

It's a given that our children will experiment with different looks, habits, music, friends, lifestyles and values. What we don't know is how far they will go with their experimentation. To what extreme will they let themselves be carried?

Setting the Limits

That's where parents, and particularly us fathers, come in. As formidable a task as it seems, it is our job to see that those limits, those boundaries, are set and enforced. We need to be the anchor that keeps our kids safe from harm amid the winds of peer pressure and childhood vulnerability.

The anchor analogy fits well. If you have a boat, you know the role an anchor plays, and how important it is to have one ready at all times. Even the slightest breeze on a calm day can send a boat floating aimlessly away. And after the breeze calms, the boat still travels from the momentum. Then another breeze comes, perhaps from a different direction, and again the boat wanders with it. It doesn't take long before you find yourself far away from your intended place on the water.

And those are just gentle breezes. Woe to the fisherman who comes upon a gale wind, sending the waves roaring and the boat heading toward the rocks. That's when you need a deep anchor—one heavy and strong enough to keep you from drifting into serious trouble.

As a boy I spent many summer afternoons water-skiing on the lake. It was my favorite sport. There's nothing more enjoyable than gliding across the top of a smooth, glassy lake. But often the winds would pick up with little notice. The waves would begin to chop, and the boat would begin rocking and taking on water. At these times, we would immediately look for a cove—a place with high rocks and ridges to block the winds. We'd park there and drop anchor, then wait for the winds to subside. It was the safest place to be, and the anchor kept us secure.

> **Three Functions of an Anchor**
> ■ *To set well-defined boundaries. Just as crucial as the weight and strength of the anchor is the amount of slack that is left after it has been dropped. If the rope is too tight—or too loose—the boat will often capsize.*
> ■ *To keep the boat from running aground or drifting off to sea. An anchor's ultimate purpose is to keep boats from crashing into the shore or drifting out into unsafe waters during times of high winds and turbulent waves.*
> ■ *To maintain the status quo. An anchor is a stabilizing force. It doesn't try to overpower the boat or drive the boat. It only serves to maintain the status quo.*

That's what an anchor does: it sets limits. It creates just enough leeway for the boat to rock and sway with the wind, but keeps it from drifting into unsafe waters.

An Anchor or a Motor?

That's how I want to view my role as a father. During times of defiance and uncertainty—times of high winds—I want to be the anchor that keeps my kids from drifting too far off center. I want to allow them the freedom to sway with the waves, but not to drift off. And like an anchor, I want to do it without fanfare, hidden far beneath the surface.

Too many times during moments of turmoil we fathers see our role as a motor. We want to fire up and drive our kids in the direction they need to go, against the changing tides—and against their wishes.

That's how Jim saw his role with his sixteen-year-old daughter, Susan. Jim and Susan were constantly at odds over even the slightest matters—how she wore her hair, how she dressed, who she was with, where they were going. He didn't like anything she did or anyone she did it with. But he never told her why. He never defined the limits; instead he arbitrarily set and enforced rules as he went. Jim didn't want to be an anchor, he wanted to be the motor—not to steady the boat, but to drive it.

During one particular shouting match Jim laid down an ultimatum. "Either you do what I say or you move out." Of course that's not what he wanted, but he had to get his point across. He wasn't prepared for what Susan did. She took her things and left, calling the next day to tell her mother not to send the police after her. "I'm in a motel, and I'm safe," she told her. "But I won't come home."

How much easier it would have been on everyone had Jim seen his job as simply to steady the boat, to keep the parameters defined, to set the limits. Instead he wanted to drive the boat, and in the process he ran it aground.

A deep anchor in a safe cove, away from the chaos of gale winds and deep waters. Giving our kids the freedom to drift, but safely monitoring the distance. Setting limits and then holding those limits fast and secure. That's how I see my role as a father during times of stress and defiance.

How Wide Is Your Circle?

Dale Darby, a good friend and local psychotherapist, once explained to me the same principle using a different analogy. He took out a napkin and drew a circle. "This circle represents the boundaries you set up for your children," he said. "It represents the limits you give them as far as what they can and can't do—their curfews, their time away from home, their freedom with friends, their dress codes, those kinds of things. As fathers we have to clearly define that circle to our kids, to make sure they understand those limits. And then we need to realize that they will be pushing those limits. Every child will eventually veer outside the circle, to see if we are willing to enforce our limits.

And if we don't, they will venture even further out.

"These boundaries, though usually met with resistance, actually give our children a great deal of security. They know their limits. And if they know we will enforce those limits, even when they push them, they feel safe and secure. They may complain and argue, but deep inside, they are happy to know where they stand."

He went on to explain that it's important not to make those limits too tight and confining. And as the children grow, the circle must be widened; their freedoms and boundaries must expand with age. But always, no matter how large the circle gets, we must hold fast in enforcing those limits. Otherwise, they will push those limits further and further, until they are no longer safe, and we no longer have the authority to bring them back into the circle.

Setting the Parameters

How do we know what limits to set? Around what parameters do we draw our circle? Again, I'd like to relinquish the floor to the experts at the Minirth-Meier clinic: "My guideline is: things that are unacceptable are illegal, immoral, permanent, or destructive behaviors. Everything that's reversible, not illegal, and not immoral is acceptable."[2]

In other words, don't draw battlelines on unimportant, unnecessary fronts.

I may not always like the newest hairstyle my kids want to try out, but within reason, I should give them freedom in that area. It's easily reversible. I may wonder about the kinds of clothes my kids want to wear, but if they are decent, not harmful or immoral, I should respect their wishes. Following the advice above, as long as their choices are not "illegal, immoral, permanent or destructive," I should back away and give them room to choose.

There are plenty of issues, of course, which do need addressing and battling over: issues that will affect their future, their reputation and their relationship with God. That's when it's time for me to step in and remind them of the rules, or the parameters of their circle, or the length of the rope to the anchor.

Like a heavy anchor in a large, unpredictable sea—that's how we should view our role as fathers in a world of fast-changing times and rushing gale winds. Survey the storm, park in the safest cove on the water, leave the right amount of slack in the rope, then drop anchor and maintain. The winds will soon pass and the waves will subside. And when they do, the boat and its passengers will be safe from harm.

A MESSAGE FOR KID-FRIENDLY MOMS

During times of childhood rebellion it is crucial that parents set clear, concise limits and then hold firmly to those limits. James Dobson likens these times to being in a rowboat during high winds. He explains that sometimes the best thing parents can do is to just sit tight and ride out the storm. If we rock the boat, we might capsize it, drowning everyone on board.

It may seem during those times that the storm will never end. But sooner or later it will pass. And if the boat is still floating, we've done our job—at least until the next storm comes along.

Nothing will rock a boat more during these times than disunity between husband and wife. When kids sense that parents are not in agreement with the rules they've laid out, it gives them incentive—and opportunity—to test those limits. If they think they have a chance of winning, they will give it all they've got. And when parents are divided on the rules of the house, the kids have every reason to believe they will win.

More than that, a disunified front confuses children as to where they stand and exactly what the rules of the house are. It makes the limits we've set seem arbitrary and negotiable. And when one rule seems that way, they begin questioning all of our rules.

It's important that you and your husband agree on the limits in your home. If you don't agree on something, talk to him in private. Negotiate a better plan of action behind closed doors. But if you want to ride out the storm, don't quibble over rules in front of the kids.

—12—
Beacon in Times
of Distress

WHEN OUR CHILDREN FIND THEMSELVES IN FRIGHTENING, UN-familiar territory, what they need most is a beacon of light to guide them back home. They need a reliable point of reference.

It was midsummer, 1979. My friends and I had been water-skiing for most of the day on Fort Phantom Lake, near Abilene, Texas. Today we had gone out on my boat—my prized possession, a bright blue speedboat with an 85-horsepower motor. Though the lake is large and winding, I knew my way around it like the back of my hand. I'd been skiing there every summer for years.

Sometime in the early evening, the winds picked up and the waves started to chop, so we pulled into a cove and waited for the winds to die down. The three of us talked and laughed and bragged about who skied the best that day, forgetting about the time and the wind. Before we knew it, the sun had nearly disappeared and it was getting darker by the minute.

Boats were not allowed on the lake after dark, so we started up the engine and headed for the dock. The winds were stronger than ever, and the darkness had caused us to lose our bearings. Lights lined the shore all around us, but we each had a different idea about which of them marked the place we had docked. As much as we hated to admit it, none of us really had a clue which way to go.

Driving at full throttle, we aimed our boat in one direction, hoping we would get lucky. We didn't. Not only that, but when we arrived near the shore, we realized we were at the opposite end of the lake from our truck and trailer. So we again aimed our boat into the dark sea, hoping the gas would last us the distance of the lake—a good twenty-minute drive at top speed. And that's in good weather.

About halfway across the lake, someone noticed that we were taking on too much water. We wondered aloud how the waves coming over the bow could accumulate so fast. Now our biggest concern was making it to shore before the boat sank—in the middle of a storm, and in the dark of night. We had no light to guide us home, and no way of knowing which direction to head. It was without a doubt the most frightening night of my life. For the first time, I worried that I wouldn't make it home alive.

To this day, I credit our survival to an alert guardian angel. We miraculously found the dock—drove right to it—and the boat somehow stayed afloat with two feet of water in its bow. (The next day we discovered we had somehow knocked a hole in the front of the boat.)

I learned that night that of all the careers I might choose for myself, becoming a sailor was out of the question. I didn't have the heart for it. I also learned about the value of lighthouses—large, bright beacons in the distance, giving a point of reference for those who found themselves in trouble. If there had been one on Fort Phantom Lake, we would have found our dock easily.

A Point of Reference

The same principle holds true for fathers and their children. When our children find themselves in frightening, unfamiliar territory, they need a beacon to guide them back home. They need a point of reference.

We fathers need to be that beacon. We need to be a true light in their lives—one that never goes dim and that can always be counted on for safe harbors.

I once had a friend named Phillip who desperately needed that kind of light in his life, but couldn't seem to find one. When he found himself in trouble, there was no light to guide him home. His father was a lot of things, but a beacon of light wasn't one of them. He worked out of town most of the time (driving a truck), and when he was home he might as well have been gone. At any rate, Phillip couldn't depend on his father to guide him.

His mother tried, but fell short. The problems in her marriage, compounded by her own self-preoccupation, left her miles apart from Phillip emotionally.

Phillip was a good kid, and for a time, a good friend. He didn't swear or drink or hang out with the wrong crowd. And he didn't go around looking for trouble. But one day, trouble found him. He was out long past the time when he should have been in bed, and with kids he never should have been allowed to hang out with. A fight broke out, a car was stolen and wrecked, and Phillip landed in jail.

That was the first time he had been locked up, but not the last. He and I had little to do with each other after that episode—something my parents saw to immediately. And he fell further and further away from home. Several years ago I inquired about him while talking to a mutual friend, and found that he had finally gone to jail for good—or at least for the better part of his life. And his parents still wonder what went wrong with Phillip.

These stories are not that uncommon. But how often do they happen to basically decent kids? I'm not sure. I knew Phillip well enough to believe that things could and should have turned out differently. All he needed was a little direction—a little guidance in his life—and he probably would have remained safe from harm.

The Power of a Guiding Light

I also once knew a boy named Brad who was probably saved when a guiding light entered his life. I know very little of the home Brad was raised in, only that at the age of thirteen the courts took him away from his natural parents and put him into a foster home. That's how he came to our town, and to the home of two wonderful Christian beacons. He lived with this couple for a few years as a foster child and then was adopted into their family.

Brad had many problems, not the least of which was a lack of discipline and direction. No one who knew him at thirteen thought he would amount to much more than a drag on a government entitlement program. With his attitude, he seemed destined for failure. But this loving couple didn't see that in him. All they saw was a boy lost in the darkness, trying desperately to find his way home.

> "*James C. Dobson, Sr. was a man of many intense loves. His greatest passion was his love for Jesus Christ. His every thought and deed were influenced by his desire to serve his Lord. And I can truthfully say that we were never together without my being drawn closer to God by simply being in my dad's presence....*
>
> "*Never once did I see him compromise with evil or abandon the faith by which he lived. His character had been like a beacon for me, illuminating my way.*"
>
> — *James Dobson, in* What My Parents Did Right, *compiled by Gloria Gaither (Nashville: Star Song, 1991), pp. 69-70.*

Over the years, a change began to occur. He slowly became less defiant, more accepting of himself and others. By the age of sixteen, he was even enjoyable to be around.

Eventually he became a Christian, started teaching Bible school classes and went on to graduate from college and enter a well-paying career.

What did Brad receive at the hands of his adoptive parents that he had never found in his previous home? He found a direction in life. A light to guide him when he strayed. He found love and acceptance. And in the end, he found his way home.

The Plane and the Firefly

When I think of what it means to be a guiding light to our children, I always think of an illustration used by author and teen counselor Joe White. In his book *Orphans at Home*, he writes of a time he was walking in a field with his daughter, Courtney, marveling at the heavens, when suddenly a jet plane cruised by. It was landing at an airport miles in the distance. As they stood watching the lights of the plane, a tiny firefly began to light up just a few feet in front of them. Immediately, he says, their attention was diverted away from the plane and toward the tiny firefly, which seemed to light up the sky around them. That's when the analogy hit him:

> For years now my [four] kids have been exposed to negative peer pressure at school, anti-family music at their friends' houses, seductive messages on television commercials—a whole assortment of modern-day bad influences. Their world is full of it, all presented in the brightest trappings to light up the eyes of children of all ages. It all looks so appealing.
>
> But I can shine my light before them. . . . I can get my little flickering flame as close as possible to their eyes, and keep that baby turned on every waking hour.
>
> My light—the steady beam of my biblical, old-fashioned, pro-family values—is small, and I can never give it the same seductive dazzle that the media fantasy-makers give their message. But I can always keep my light just a whisper away from those four precious pairs of eyes, as they look for leadership and direction.[1]

I like that analogy, especially since I know my own limitations. In a world of razzle-dazzle excitement, I may seem like little more than a firefly to my children. It's comforting to know that's all I need to be. That my firefly-light is bright enough to gain their attention and guide their way. But only if I'm willing to keep shining, to keep glowing, and to stay close enough to their eyes to fill their world with light.

The Power of Consistency

Another valuable characteristic of a lighthouse is its consistency.

A few years ago, while visiting relatives on the East Coast, we took a drive up to Rhode Island and had lunch at the foot of a lighthouse. I was surprised by its size, and especially at the size of its beam. But more than that, I was amazed to find how consistent this lighthouse had been over the years. A plaque at the base told when the lighthouse was built and the date its beam first shot out over the ocean. Though I don't remember the exact dates, it had been shining for many years. And in that time, the light had never once stopped shining. Never once had its beam gone dim. Through storms, high winds, hurricanes, even major repairs to the lighthouse foundation, the beacon had never stopped shining out over the ocean, guiding lost sailors home.

That's the kind of consistency that I want to have. I don't want to ever let my light fade or waver for even a moment. I want to shine bright and long and true, and to never give up.

Just this week in the news we've been hearing about a woman in Louisiana who has filed a petition to divorce her three teenage daughters. "I'm just tired of being a mother," she explained to the media. "They don't listen to me anyway. No matter what I say they do what they want to do. I have all the worries, all the financial burden of raising them, all the headaches, but no reward for myself. I want to do something for myself for a change."

There's nothing more pathetic than a quitter, especially when it comes to parenting. If you're going to take a cue, don't take it from this woman. Take it instead from a lighthouse. And from a man named Jeffrey.

Jeffrey has three great kids. They are all faithful to him and to God. But there was a time not so long ago when you couldn't say that. One of his kids, Drake, wasn't always such a good kid. In fact he was far from it.

The wrong crowd in high school got him involved in the wrong lifestyle, and before he knew it he was hooked on everything from sex to alcohol to drugs to every other vice you could imagine. No one believed Drake would ever be able to find his way back home.

Except Jeffrey. He never gave up. Never stopped shining. Never quit throwing his light in Drake's direction, beckoning him to aim for safe harbors.

Some thought that Jeffrey was being an "enabler" to his son, but only those who weren't close to the situation. There was no question in Drake's mind where his father stood on his sinful life, nor did he ever wonder under what conditions he would be accepted back. There would be no acceptance of his lifestyle or his friends or his bad habits. Not in Jeffrey's house. But Drake—clean and sober—was always welcome. The light was always there if he needed it.

> *I would love to hear any comments or questions you might have concerning this book. I'd also enjoy hearing any family stories or anecdotes you may have from your own experiences as a parent.*
>
> *Feel free to write to me:*
>
> **Frank Martin**
> **6610 Bugle Drive**
> **Colorado Springs, CO 80918**

This was a case of tough love in its extreme. And though even James Dobson, popularizer of the idea and author of the book *Tough Love,* will tell you that it doesn't always work out, in Drake's case it did. After years of fighting, Drake came home and docked in safe waters for good.

Jeffrey could have given up. In fact I'm sure he felt like it many times. But he didn't. He never turned away, never let his beacon wane, and his commitment and consistency eventually paid off.

A Light That Never Goes Out

When it comes to my kids, I want them to know that they always have a place to go in times of distress. I want them to know that no matter how hectic and exciting and bright the lights of the world shine around them, there is always one light that will be there when all the others have faded. There is one harbor where they will always be safe from harm. And standing there is the one beacon of light that shines for them above all others—one that marks the dock that is always safe and secure.

Last week we took our children to see Big Bird and the Sesame Street Live program at the Civic Center downtown. David sat waving his balloon and jumping up and down in his seat, while Kandilyn, our ten-month-old, sat in my lap. David has been to this show before—too many times—but this was Kandilyn's first time.

As the show started, the lights went dim, the music played loud and the spotlights lit up the stage with excitement. Kids all around us started screaming and clapping in anticipation. It was an intense moment, and I felt Kandilyn's little body stiffen up. I could sense she was about to start crying, so I turned her around to face me. "Daddy's here, Kandilyn," I told her. "Don't worry—Daddy's here."

I could see the fear in her eyes as I tried to get her attention. "Kandilyn, don't be afraid. Daddy's got you."

Then she caught a glimpse of my face, and her eyes lit up. She smiled widely and waved her arms in excitement.

Suddenly, everything was all right. I turned her back around, and together we sat watching the show. Every now and then she would glance up to make sure I was still there. I'd smile, she'd smile back, and then she'd turn again to watch the excitement.

I hope this is one part of our relationship that never changes. I hope she always looks in my direction when life gets loud and dark and intense, making sure I'm still shining. And when she does, I'll be there.

You can bet the farm on that.

Notes

Chapter 2: Father-in-Residence
[1]Tim Hansel, *What Kids Need Most in a Dad* (Old Tappan, N.J.: Revell, 1984), p. 165.
[2]"How Americans Are Running Out of Time," *Time*, April 24, 1989, pp. 74-76.

Chapter 3: Spiritual Shepherd
[1]Jorie L. Kincaid, *The Power of Modeling* (Colorado Springs, Colo.: NavPress, 1989), pp. 15, 22.

Chapter 4: Image Consultant
[1]Robert G. Barnes Jr., *Raising Confident Kids* (Grand Rapids, Mich.: Zondervan, 1992), pp. 30-31.
[2]Josh McDowell and Norm Wakefield, *The Dad Difference* (San Bernardino, Calf.: Here's Life Publishers, 1989).
[3]Barnes, *Raising Confident Kids*, p. 35.

Chapter 5: Financial Adviser
[1]James Patterson and Peter Kim, *The Day America Told the Truth* (New York: Prentice Hall, 1991), pp. 45-46.

Chapter 6: Career Guidance Counselor
[1]Jerry B. Jenkins, *Twelve Things I Want My Kids to Remember Forever* (Chicago: Moody Press, 1991), p. 30.
[2]*Christian Ministry*, January 1979, p. 26.

Chapter 7: Shop Teacher
[1]Joe White, *Orphans at Home* (Phoenix, Ariz.: Questar, 1988), pp. 138-39.

Chapter 10: Model of Masculinity
[1]Bill McCartney, *What Makes a Man?* (Colorado Springs, Colo.: NavPress, 1992), pp. 11-12.
[2]Lee Haines, in *Wesleyan Advocate,* June 9, 1975, p. 6.

Chapter 11: Anchor in Times of Defiance
[1]Frank Minirth, Brian Newman and Paul Warren, *The Father Book* (Nashville: Thomas Nelson, 1992), pp. 160-61, 165.
[2]Ibid., p. 165.

Chapter 12: Beacon in Times of Distress
[1]White, *Orphans at Home,* p. 49.